Further praise for *Engaging Data*

"*Engaging Data* is more than another academic recitation of public relations principles. Trinette Marquis has provided the principles of PR in a way that is approachable and easily digestible for any practitioner, whether they have been working in school PR for two decades or two weeks. But more than making the principles approachable, Trinette has provided examples that bring the principles to life—something that is so often lacking from PR texts. She demonstrates how data can transform the practice of PR so that it is impacting student learning. I've attended numerous sessions Trinette has presented at national conferences and had great success implementing the very practices outlined in this book. I urge every school PR professional to run to their local bookseller and pick up a copy. You will not be disappointed. In fact, you just may find that your practice is more organized and effective at achieving measured goals."
— **Krystyna M. Baumgartner, public relations specialist, Bay Shore Union Free School District**

"Without data to inform public relations, you have no foundation for the communications 'house' you're trying to build for your school district. Things will fall apart fast. Author and school public relations expert Trinette Marquis makes this case for all public relations professionals in 'Data-Driven PR,' a well-stocked guide to demographics, psychographics, RACE, metrics, user flow, click rates, Google Analytics, Facebook Insights, and more. If you're not familiar with these terms and haven't yet discovered the value of data to inform the way you work, then this book is for you."
— **Evelyn McCormack, president, Mack Digital Communications**

"Have you ever asked yourself what you should do about a problem or how you'll know if your efforts are successful? Trinette Marquis can help you answer those and many other questions. The consummate data geek, her passion for research and data-driven decision making is infectious. As a teacher and a professional, Trinette provides creative ways to conduct research that help overcome budget, staffing, and resource shortfalls so that your campaign launches with solid data and collects the information you'll need to measure its effectiveness."
— **Trent Allen, APR, senior director of community relations, San Juan Unified School District and past president, Public Relations Society of America, California Capital Chapter**

"This book is a must-have for any school PR practitioner. Whether you are a one-person shop who is new to the field or a seasoned professional with a team of resources at your disposal, the knowledge and insight into effectively collecting and using data will be invaluable additions to your communications toolbox. This book is a perfect example of why Trinette is a well-known and respected authority in data-driven communications and leadership. She offers readers a detailed look at the importance of using data to drive communication efforts and provides easy-to-understand processes for collecting, analyzing, and utilizing data to better support the schools and communities you serve."
— **Curtis Campbell, public information officer, Shoreline Public Schools (Shoreline, Washington); past president, Washington School Public Relations Association**

Engaging Data

Engaging Data

Smart Strategies for School Communication

Trinette Marquis, APR

Published in Partnership with the
National School Public Relations Association

ROWMAN & LITTLEFIELD
Lanham • Boulder • New York • London

Published in Partnership with the National School Public Relations Association

Published by Rowman & Littlefield
An imprint of The Rowman & Littlefield Publishing Group, Inc.
4501 Forbes Boulevard, Suite 200, Lanham, Maryland 20706
www.rowman.com

Unit A, Whitacre Mews, 26-34 Stannary Street, London SE11 4AB, United Kingdom

Copyright © 2018 by Trinette Marquis

All rights reserved. No part of this book may be reproduced in any form or by any electronic or mechanical means, including information storage and retrieval systems, without written permission from the publisher, except by a reviewer who may quote passages in a review.

British Library Cataloguing in Publication Information Available

Library of Congress Cataloging-in-Publication Data

Names: Marquis, Trinette, author.
Title: Engaging data : smart strategies for school communication / Trinette Marquis.
Description: Lanham, Maryland : Rowman & Littlefield, [2018] | Includes bibliographical references.
Identifiers: LCCN 2018006504 (print) | LCCN 2018022579 (ebook) | ISBN 9781475841893 (Electronic) | ISBN 9781475841879 (cloth : alk. paper) | ISBN 9781475841886 (pbk. : alk. paper)
Subjects: LCSH: Schools—Public relations—United States. | Communication in education—United States. | Education—United States—Data processing.
Classification: LCC LB2847 (ebook) | LCC LB2847 .M38 2018 (print) | DDC 371.102/2—dc23
LC record available at https://lccn.loc.gov/2018006504

In 2006 when I left the technology sector and a hefty salary to go and work in my hometown school system, everyone in my life (with the exception of my dad who was still a custodian there) told me it was a mistake.

It was one of the few times I followed my gut instead of the data, and I've never regretted the decision—even on the toughest of days.

I never expected to learn so much from my fellow school leaders and communicators. The people I've connected with at the California School Public Relations Association and the National School Public Relations Association are among the best in the public relations field in any industry.

They are sharp, kind, creative, and mission-driven. They are the conscience of their organizations and a voice for those who can't speak loudly enough for themselves. I'm proud to be one of them. This book is dedicated to everyone serving in a school communication role.

"Life is mostly froth and bubble, two things stand like stone. Kindness in another's trouble, courage in your own."

—Adam Lindsay Gordon

Contents

Foreword		xi
Preface		xv
Acknowledgments		xvii
Introduction		xix
1	The Case for Data	1
2	The Four-Step Public Relations Process	11
3	Research, Easier than You Might Think	19
4	Data, Data Everywhere	25
5	Designing Surveys that Truly Listen	31
6	What Gets Measured Gets Done: Creating Accountability	41
7	Analytics, the Low-Hanging Data Fruit	49
8	Low(er) Tech Tracking Ideas	59
9	Making Data Accessible	65
10	Qualitative Research, Understanding the Richness of Experience	71
11	When the Data Is Hard to Swallow	79
12	No PR Person, No Problem!	85

Appendix A	Sample Communication Plan	97
Appendix B	Sample Communication Survey Questions	103
Appendix C	Training Ideas to Expand Communications Function	107
Appendix D	Four-Step Process Campaign Example	109
Appendix E	Communication Options Worksheet	113
Glossary		115
Resources		117
About the Author		119

Foreword

Before we start, it should be noted: I hear voices.

Out of context, this sounds mildly psychotic. It's important, though, because many days those voices are Trinette's.

I'll back up and explain a little more.

A long time ago, I was a newspaper scribe scribbling three to five stories a week about the communities I covered. When my pieces ran, I hoped readers would care. I rarely knew if they did. My job performance wasn't judged on that anyway; my editors cared more about how many times my byline appeared on page A1. I did, too, if we're being honest.

Fast-forward a few years, and like a lot of newsroom refugees, I found myself navigating a new and rewarding career in public relations. I couldn't wait to take on long-term marketing projects and strategic communication plans to show off just how many brilliant ideas I had. Flashy fliers, photo galleries, witty Twitter posts, epic videos, let's do this!

Then I started meeting people like Trinette Marquis, who appeared to derive pleasure from hearing my ideas and then asking questions like, "OK, but what evidence will tell us we've succeeded?" or, "It's an interesting tactic, but how does it address what our stakeholders have been telling us?" and, naturally, "What exactly are we hoping to achieve?"

Ouch.

She was right, though. What's a project's worth without a clear purpose? You do need evidence to know your impact. However, this seemed daunting. I was a communications major, not a statistician. How was I supposed to rewire my writerly brain to crunch numbers?

It turns out that I didn't have to. Here's the thing I've learned from Trinette: I was missing the point. Doing the research can be as creative an act as crafting the message.

In our work, we are surrounded by easy-to-collect evidence—if we pause to look. Existing surveys that we can sprinkle in targeted questions, for instance. Focus groups curated from the community groups with whom we strive to connect. Employee directories you can use to cross-reference names in the comments thread of Facebook posts (who knew so many of your staffers were stirring things up!). I work in public schools; how many freaking sign-in sheets do we use on a daily basis? How about we strategically sneak some metrics into those?

Over the years, through her steady and supportive guidance, Trinette has trained me and countless other young professionals to ask these kinds of questions daily. It's why I'm so thrilled to see her unique expertise published on these pages.

(It's also why I hear her voice in the back of my head during most days. See? Not psychotic.)

Whether you're a public relations professional or someone at the school or district level taking on communication and engagement, this book will give you the foundation (or refresher) you need to continue doing your best work. No matter whether you have a couple of days to craft a comprehensive, color-coded plan, or you're running out the door with some back-of-the-napkin notes, we should be approaching every project with the simple questions: What do we want people to think or do? How will we make sure they do? How will we know if they did?

A valuable by-product of doing better work? Demonstrating your value every day.

If you can meaningfully measure what you do, over time there will be far fewer people in your organization inclined to ask, "What if we just made a brochure," or, even worse, "Just what does this communications person do all day?" Many leadership teams take for granted the role of communication strategists for the volume of outputs they can easily see: social media campaigns, viral videos, on-message media interviews, or award-winning ads. Sure, all of these things are necessary, most of the time. But in the end, can your employer add all these tactics up and show how they moved your organization closer to meeting your highest-priority goals?

Trinette's book unpacks the myriad ways we can measure our impact with the same thought and care she devotes to her craft, her clients, her students, and to the countless young professionals (like me) she has generously mentored throughout her career. Truly take the time to savor her words and scrawl in the margins.

In short, this is the book I wish had within reach of my desk years ago.

Daniel Thigpen
Director, Communication & Community Engagement
Folsom Cordova Unified School District
President, Public Relations Society of America California Capital Chapter
Past President, California School Public Relations Association

Preface

Growing up, one television show in particular drove me crazy. Every week on *Three's Company*, Jack Tripper would eavesdrop on Janet Wood talking to a friend (or some similar scenario with different characters) and make an assumption about what it meant.

The rest of the thirty minutes would involve all of the characters acting out elaborate schemes based on the misinterpretation—instead of just communicating with each other.

While the opening misinterpretation would vary slightly, the resulting chaos was the same. As I watched, I would grow more and more frustrated, sometimes balling up my ten-year-old fists and yelling at the ridiculous roommates to "just talk to each other!"

I credit the show with igniting my passion for effective communication and starting me on the path to an extremely varied and rewarding career, and eventually, this book.

There were definitely some bumps along the way. While I am affectionately known by my public relations colleagues as the "data geek," it hasn't always been this way. I took just one math class in my undergraduate program and barely passed.

When I was required to take several research classes in my master's program, I was intrigued and tested several of the methods in my communication roles with a variety of organizations.

Later, going through the accreditation process for public relations—especially studying research and evaluation—I was hooked. It was like I received a new lens with which to view communication.

My work for clients became much more focused, and the results were thrilling to see. I began presenting to my state and national colleagues about the importance of data, documenting all the tips and tricks I've used, and eventually committed to writing it all down to share more broadly.

Whether you're a PR pro, a principal, a school counselor, or a superintendent, my hope is that this book will give you at least one idea that saves you time and improves communication (hopefully a lot more than one!)—and I'd truly love to hear about it if it does.

Within each chapter, I've included commonsense reasons to incorporate data practices as well as practical examples and templates to put them immediately to work, even if you're not a data person.

Writing this book was an incredible learning experience that coincidentally put me in touch with many of the methods described in these chapters. On the qualitative research side, I got to interview a number of seasoned and talented school communicators, hearing about the ways they have put data to work for their districts and schools.

The title of the book? Ideas crowdsourced from PR colleagues and narrowed through a survey of target audience representatives.

So, dear reader, thank you for the work you do that led you to this book, and more than anything, I hope to help you increase engagement, trust, and support in public schools. They *are* the great equalizer and foundation of our democratic ideals, and they deserve our time, talent, and energy.

Acknowledgments

Many people contributed to this project in ways both large and small, but all played a part. My dad and sisters are my foundation. They are my biggest cheerleaders, helping me believe I can do anything I set out to do. I wish more of our young people had that kind of support at home.

As a bigger geek than me, my hubby, Ken, challenges me to bring my best to everything. He can see right through a less-than-stellar effort on my part, and when I earn his praise, I know I deserve it. I found myself writing as if Ken were looking over my shoulder.

School has always been my sanctuary. No matter what else was happening in life, there were people in elementary school, junior high, high school, and college who helped me reframe what was happening and allow me to focus on learning. I am immensely grateful to the staff and teachers at Katherine Finchy Elementary in Palm Springs and FC Joyce Elementary, Don Julio Junior High, and Highlands High School in North Highlands, California.

My greatest influences at CSU Sacramento—professors Barbara O'Connor, Gerri Smith, Marlene von Friederichs-Fitzwater, Nick Trujillo, Kimo Ah Yun, and Val Smith—focused and fueled my love for communication research and theory.

In one of my first professional roles, good friend Regino Chavez, qualitative research guru, inspired a passion for truly listening to the people you want to serve. He also helped a great deal with the qualitative research sections of this book.

Former boss Frank Porter gave me the freedom and (extreme!) challenges to discover how much I could grow professionally. Despite dealing with some incredibly difficult situations, I wouldn't trade the experience for anything.

Bestie Kate inspires me to ask the tough questions and to stay student-focused. She is relentlessly honest, which has helped me grow into a person who cares more about what the data says than whether or not I am liked.

Trent is my partner in all things school PR, literally "tricking" me into state board service and always encouraging me to take on greater challenges. He is the competitive, caring, crazy brother I was lucky enough to get later in life.

Since going out on my own, I have been blessed with an array of client projects that have allowed me to see school communication from completely new perspectives. From large urban to small rural districts, the stakeholder research and campaign implementation gave me the confidence to write something that I believe will be universally helpful.

Having worked in PR in several major industries, I can say without qualification that the best in any field are in education. As is typical with generous and talented school communicator types, when word got out that I was working on this project, a number stood up and said, "Whatever you need."

This list includes (in alphabetical order): Angela, Carla, Curtis, Dan, Evelyn, Heidi, Julie, Kelly, Krystyna, Lesley, Music, Nicole, Nora, and Sandy. Your time, experience, and wisdom contributed so much to make this happen. From case studies to editing to endorsements, each one jumped in to help out.

Last and certainly not least, a huge thanks to my friend and colleague Kristin who got this thing rolling by telling me (again and again) that I could write a book—and showing me how it's done.

Introduction

WHY THIS BOOK?

We are very familiar with using data in school systems. We can tell you which third grader needs a reading intervention to get them up to grade level, how many lunches are served in a given day, how many miles our buses drive each year, and how many computers are in our middle school lab.

For some reason though, that data-driven perspective hasn't made it into most of our communication efforts. We have been fairly comfortable in making PR decisions on the basis of "knowing our community" or because it is "what we have always done."

We wouldn't want our classroom teachers approaching student learning without assessing where students are starting and how well their teaching methods are working—we shouldn't expect anything less in our communication efforts.

The fact is that approaching your PR planning without the foundational data is like cutting the front lawn with a dull pair of scissors. Communication can still occur, but there is a lot of wasted time and effort.

This book is intended to provide a new focus for the seasoned school PR pro and general guidance for the school or district leader doing the communications work as part of another job. In both cases, these chapters will provide a number of tips, templates, and resources to save you time and help you be more effective in your efforts.

HOW TO USE THIS BOOK

Whether you're a seasoned PR pro or have taken on communication and engagement for your school or district, this book was written with you in mind. Whether you're excited about the opportunity to integrate data into your communications work or you're a little apprehensive about the idea, this book has you covered.

From cheap and easy research methods, to tips for survey development, to systemic tracking and reporting ideas that will demonstrate the value of communication, it's in here. This book is not an attempt to develop professional researchers but to demonstrate in a variety of ways how a few basic research strategies can give you the confidence to master data-driven engagement and increase the likelihood of meeting your communication objectives.

We'll cover everything you need to build a solid communication plan, easy research methods and data sources to tap into, and simple tracking and measuring tools that will help you demonstrate and report the value of communication and engagement. It was written in a way that allows the reader to visit particular chapters of interest or to leisurely read from cover-to-cover.

CHAPTERS 1 AND 2: SETTING THE STAGE

In the first chapter, we'll discuss the need for data and where it fits in PR. We'll cover the three key areas in which data must be utilized to create effective communication campaigns. We'll also learn from a veteran PR pro about her experience in moving from one large school system to another—while the systems shared similar challenges, her approach to them was very different because of the data.

Chapter 2 will review the four-step PR process that is the gold standard in the industry and break it down into easy-to-understand steps that anyone can implement. While all four steps are important, we'll go in-depth on research and evaluation, the first and last steps in the process that are greatly impacted by the collection and analysis of good data.

A case study in Chapter 2 will take us to Tuscaloosa, Alabama, to find out how data helped a school district recruit and retain quality bus drivers. A second study describes the change in a communications office that happens when the four-step process becomes part of the culture. There is also a handy table covering the four-step process with specific questions and ideas under each one to help guide your planning.

CHAPTERS 3, 4, AND 5: COLLECTING THE DATA

In the third chapter, we'll explore the different kinds of research and review specific-to-schools examples under each one. A research case study will show how budget cuts guided by input can go more smoothly, and a second will demonstrate how a PR pro used research to save the district $20,000 while making employees feel better appreciated.

Chapter 4 is all about simplifying the process of collecting data. There are dozens of ways that schools and districts are already collecting information that can help guide communication. We'll identify them and provide some data-collecting "hacks" to make it even easier to get the information you need. The data case study is about a district in California that lets their audience communication preferences guide their advertising dollars.

If the idea of developing a survey gives you the willies, Chapter 5 will be a lifesaver. It will be a very detailed dive into what makes the best surveys work—how to write them, format them, organize them, and market them to learn all you need to know about your audiences. There are several example questions and even a list of tips to use for your next survey effort.

A district in Missouri is the subject of the chapter's case study. Their seasoned director of communication shares the top two questions they ask every year that tell them the most about their community.

CHAPTERS 6, 7, AND 8: IT'S ALL ABOUT MEASURING

Chapter 6 covers what may be the most difficult piece to master in developing an effective communication campaign—creating measurable objectives. However, if we're not developing campaigns with the end in mind, we can get off track. Measurable objectives make campaign planning much easier—you only include the activities that will help you meet your objectives.

We'll break them down into their key elements and explore a variety of examples related to schools. You'll also learn what steps to take when you're in a situation when, for a number of reasons, you're not able to set a measurable objective.

In Chapter 7, analytics are the focus. We'll specifically take a look at some of the most common systems that schools are using, like websites, social media, and e-newsletters, and review how the data can be pulled and analyzed.

One of the Chapter 7 case studies will describe how one district put analytics to work in addressing community concerns about an eclipse their classrooms used to teach science.

Chapter 8 gets away from the technical to focus on some of my favorite, commonsense ways to start tracking the amount of communications activity that takes place in a school or district. Don't worry, these are super-easy and won't add a lot to your day—they will add the proof that your day is much fuller than anyone imagined.

CHAPTER 9: EXPLAIN THE NUMBERS

Once we've gotten good at finding and setting up systems to continue tracking all the data, it doesn't do us any good if it doesn't get reported in a way that people can understand. In Chapter 9, we'll be discussing strategies to make large numbers easier to comprehend for families and other stakeholders.

This will include a discussion of helpful analogies, graphics, and infographics to highlight the most important statistics, as well as tools we can use to create them. It will also cover ideas for reporting the numbers—ensuring the broader community understands the value of the work that is being done on their behalf.

CHAPTER 10: DON'T FORGET QUALITATIVE RESEARCH

This chapter was added after realizing that all the other chapters, while discussing data as a whole, mostly focus on quantitative methods. Chapter 10 discusses a number of qualitative research methods that school leaders can undertake to gain a richer understanding of a given issue.

There are also two interesting case studies as part of the chapter. One describes how a clever PR person from a New York area district bartered with another local agency to get independent focus group facilitators for them both. The second case study focuses on a district in Canada that shrewdly makes a special effort to develop what they call "critical friends"—stakeholders that will provide much needed qualitative feedback, even when it's negative.

CHAPTER 11: THAT'S NOT WHAT I EXPECTED

Sometimes when the data comes back, it doesn't support continuing down a path that a school or district is already on. This chapter will investigate the steps available when the unexpected happens, from additional research to confirm the results to using the results to forge a new way forward.

The chapter case studies highlight two districts that used the data to change course for their communication efforts, saving them a lot of time and resources.

CHAPTER 12: NO PR PERSON? NO PROBLEM!

This last chapter is for everyone reading this book who has taken on PR as part of their regular job. Don't worry, it can be done, and we'll discuss how. The first part of Chapter 12 covers a few ideas that other districts have implemented to share the workload and ensure that everyone feels that communication is everyone's job.

The second half covers one of the biggest challenges facing smaller districts and schools—how to add social media to an already busy day. You can access twenty-five posting ideas, practical tips to consider in managing social media, and a sample content calendar to help you organize all of your posts.

SPECIAL SECTIONS

This book includes a few extra sections after the chapters. They include a glossary, a resources page, and five templates (Appendices A through E). The glossary is a list of PR and data-related terms with definitions related to how they are used in this book. This would be a very useful first section for non-PR or new PR staff.

The resources page includes a short list of organizations, websites, and books for additional information. It also includes a number of ways to connect with me online.

The templates are a special bonus, sample documents that can inspire schools and districts to get started right away. There is a sample communication plan (Appendix A), sample communication preferences survey (Appendix B), a list of suggested staff training topics (Appendix C), an in-depth look at a district's successful campaign (Appendix D), and a template for collecting school communication tools on one page for easy communication planning (Appendix E).

GET READING!

Each chapter contains my best advice in each area, graphics or tables to make the material easier to understand, and example templates to help you get started right away. Don't have time to read the full chapter or not sure if it will cover a topic that you need? Skip to the end and check out the key ideas near the end of each one for a bulleted list of the major categories of information that were discussed.

The chapter case studies highlight examples around the country and provide a richer understanding of how the tips provided in this book make a difference in everyday school situations.

And with that, I leave you to Chapter 1, the case for data.

Chapter One

The Case for Data

"It is a capital mistake to theorize before one has data."

—Sherlock Holmes

Imagine going on a hike without knowing anything about it. You don't know how long it is, what the elevation is, or even what the weather is. When you don't know where you are headed, how long it may take, or what the conditions may be, you expend a lot of energy and resources on things that don't matter or even things that get in the way.

You might bring a jacket that ends up tied around your waist in eighty-degree weather, be forced to lug several bottles of water for a trip that only lasts a couple of hours, or forget to bring bug spray when the mosquitos are out. Most people would never dream of setting off on a hike without knowing a lot of information about where they are going and the conditions of their trip.

Yet that is exactly what happens when we decide to communicate without the data. When we decide to create a communication campaign and don't think through what our success will look like (our destination) or about the audiences, tools, and messages (conditions), we will waste a lot of time and energy on things that don't matter.

PR PEOPLE DON'T DO DATA

When people think about communication and public relations (PR), they may think that it is a purely creative field meant for people who are mostly right-brained and artistic. They imagine the best PR people simply have an innate and mysterious talent for knowing exactly what to say and when to say it.

There is some truth to that perspective. Most people who work in communication and PR do have a way with words, but many times what feeds that skill is a great deal of experience in which they are unintentionally storing away data about what works and what doesn't work with a variety of audiences.

The best in the field make that data gathering creative and explicit, searching out new information and reviewing even the most inspired ideas with potential audiences and trusted advisors. They are true lifelong learners because every campaign is a new set of circumstances to explore and understand.

Not a communication or PR professional? Not a problem. Any school leader that has an interest in improving communication at a school or campus can and should put the same data to work in their efforts. In Chapter 12, you'll learn specific strategies and tactics for schools and districts without a communication professional.

TWO HALVES

While it may seem that there is little connection between creative PR tactics and the gathering and use of data, they are two halves of the development of highly effective campaigns.

It's not so different from the way the human brain operates. The left side of our brain performs tasks that have to do with analytic thought and logic, like science and mathematics.

On the other hand, the right hemisphere of our brain performs tasks that have to do with imagination, intuition, and creativity. While many people may be more comfortable or lean more heavily to one side or the other, we unconsciously call on both parts of our brain each day.

Effective communication planning requires us to do that more explicitly. We must use data to fully understand the nature of a challenge or opportunity, demonstrate the most powerful tools to use for specific audiences, and track and evaluate our efforts so that we continue to improve our practice.

We also bring in our intuition and creativity, which combined with the information we've collected, results in targeted, sincere, student-centered messaging that cuts through the noise and reaches the hearts and minds of our audiences.

It is similar to the data-driven approach in improving student learning outcomes in classrooms. Table 1.1 provides a quick reference to the types of questions data can help answer.

Table 1.1.

Data Helps Us Understand the Issue and Plan to Effectively Address It	
Who are your audiences?	Most impacted
	Most influential
What do you know about them?	Preferences
	Concerns
	Demographics
How will you know if you're successful?	Feedback
	Behavior

UNDERSTANDING THE ISSUE

When a challenge or opportunity is presented to a school community, it is tempting to jump in and to want to develop a quick fix, especially when someone in leadership is demanding exactly that.

For example, a school board member steps into the office and announces, "We have an urgent issue! Parents are very, very upset about the switch to 2% milk! We have to do something!"

The PR person or the person conducting that work (many times included as other duties are assigned) should take the time to investigate the nature and scope of the issue. It could look something like this:

> The person charged with PR: "OK, let's talk about this for a minute. I want to understand who is upset and why. How many calls or emails have you received about this?"
>
> Board member: "I got two calls over the weekend, and they said everyone is complaining about the change."
>
> The person charged with PR: "OK, I'm going to put this on our radar to track and let's check in again tomorrow [or later in the week depending on the board member's patience level] to discuss our options for addressing the issue. In the meantime, please provide me with contact information, and I will reach out and talk with them about the issue."

The board member leaves the office knowing that you take the issue seriously, that you are putting in additional effort to discover the scope of the problem, and that you'll be responsive in a way that is appropriate to the issue.

If you discover it really is causing widespread alarm in the community, there will be some options to consider. You can reverse the decision, put together an informational campaign about the change, or something in between.

Your data about the communication preferences of your audiences will be one of the first places to turn to communicate with families about the district's understanding of the issue and their intentions. Do they get most of their information from a school-based email? Make sure that is at the top of the list of communication tools if you need to reach out.

On the other hand, if you discover that only two calls were coming from parents and that those calls were encouraged by a staff person because the staff personally wanted to be able to access the 2% milk, you have a completely different communication issue to explore.

If you don't take the time to collect the data about an issue, it is impossible to understand what to do next with any confidence.

A great benefit to this approach is that once data-driven communication becomes the norm, staff members may even begin to adjust and start to collect information themselves to determine the nature of the issue.

If they are well-trained, they can ask a lot more qualifying questions when an item comes up. This has the potential to cut down on the number of issues that make it to the level that requires a school leader or communication professional.

UNDERSTANDING THE AUDIENCES

Once the nature of the issue is understood, data can also help with identifying the key audiences. Who is the most impacted by the issue? Who is influential with those who are impacted? Who does the impacted audience trust? All of these are questions that quantitative and qualitative research can answer.

Enrollment information, census data, and survey responses can tell us a lot about how many people we are trying to reach, where they live, where they send their children to school, and if they even have children.

Focus groups talking about the issue at hand or influential sources of information in their world can tell us a lot about the messages and sources that are likely to be most effective.

For example, several years ago, in and around districts throughout the country, there was a spate of school vandalism, specifically thieves that wanted to strip the copper out of the heating and air-conditioning systems. The repairs and new systems cost schools millions of dollars.

In planning a campaign to ask the neighboring community to help watch the school after hours, we might look to quantitative data to understand more about the potential audiences. In many school neighborhoods, there are older homes with people whose children left long ago.

Relying on a voicemail call to families would likely not reach the audiences most able to assist. If a campaign is implemented without thinking through the audiences, we can spend a lot of time and energy on things that don't reach the right people.

After identifying the key audiences and influencers, we need to understand the best ways to reach them. While messages are important and identifying audiences is critical, determining communication preferences is like building the bridge between the two.

A message that is not sent out through the right channel is a lot less likely to reach the target. Paying attention to the analytics on communication systems or asking audiences to self-report their preferences can provide detailed information about how to maximize the effectiveness of the effort.

In the case above of trying to recruit neighbors to assist with watching the school, a great qualitative method, such as an interview with a homeowner near the school, may reveal the best tools for the audience. Perhaps an announcement at the next senior center bingo night will hit the bull's-eye and keep the copper where it belongs.

MEASURING CAMPAIGN EFFORTS

During and after the communication campaign, how do you know if you are successful? Without data, we must rely on anecdotal information from people who are likely already connected to the school and district, reinforcing the things we usually do. Data helps us to get outside of our feedback bubble and hear from people that we may not be as connected with.

If a Facebook post is lackluster, the data might show us that posts with photos or videos perform much better with our audiences that use social media. If enrollment isn't growing as fast as we expected, the data might show that a significant portion of our potential student population isn't online and needs to be reached in a different way.

Lesley Bruinton, the public relations coordinator of Tuscaloosa City Schools, considers data her "rumble strip" during a campaign. If the strategies and tactics are the roads, the data tells her if a campaign has gotten off track in some way, and it gives her an opportunity to correct during the drive.

Once the campaign is over, data is just as important. If we've set a measurable objective, as will be explained in Chapter 6, there is a feedback or behavior target we were striving for in the campaign.

For example, the number of new students enrolled in a program, a percentage growth in positive perception of the district, or a percentage decrease in missed school days. Analyzing our results against the objective, the simple answer of meeting or missing the target, is easy. What's harder is looking at the reasons why—and that is where the deeper data dive comes in.

Beyond the benefits of communication planning, collecting data allows us to stop guessing and make informed decisions in all areas. Instead of sitting in a leadership meeting and debating each other's potentially flawed approach, data shows us the way forward.

It helps us focus our limited time and energy on the things that matter. If one item is a much bigger issue affecting the broader community than another that is a pet project, data gives us the argument to focus on the more important issue. If something isn't working or is no longer a helpful communication tool, data gives us the evidence we need to move from one tool to another.

REVEALING TRENDS AND THEMES

One thing that happens when we continually collect information across years and across systems is that we can begin to make comparisons. Is there one school that seems to get a lot more media attention? An interview with their administrator may reveal that their librarian has a passion for getting the word out about the program.

What specifically is the librarian doing and how can you make it systematic? What training and equipment are needed at the other schools so that they are receiving the same kind of positive attention?

It can also allow you to predict what may be happening in the community. Looking at survey results about communication preferences over several years in a row is likely to provide a lot of insight about the tools that are growing in popularity and reach and those that are waning.

In 2005, automated voice calls to families were incredibly helpful and effective. Unlike the internet, most people had access to a home or mobile phone and could receive information about as quickly as a school could record it.

If for some reason school was canceled for the day, families were informed well before students set out, saving everyone a lot of time and likely keeping a lot of kids safe.

As of the writing of this book, many schools and districts are seeing the popularity of this tool fall. It seems in this time of extreme busyness, no one has the time to listen all the way through a voicemail. With the proliferation of smartphone technology, most people can get a text or email on their mobile phones even more quickly.

When putting those two data points together, what can we predict for the future? If people feel impatient about listening to a two-minute voicemail, what are the implications for written material?

When evaluating potential tools for campaigns, which are most likely to be effective? It will probably be those that are fast and efficient, meeting the expectations of our audience's shrinking attention spans.

The most valuable trends that can be uncovered through data are the biases in our system. While nearly everyone in a school system goes into that work for all the right reasons, we bring our life experiences in the door with us. Those life experiences can turn into unintentional bias at the personal level, and it sometimes rises to the systemic level.

On a day-to-day basis, it may not even occur to someone that they are acting with bias, but over time, the data can reveal it. In communication efforts, it may come up as highlighting the schools and programs that are run by friends or are in certain neighborhoods.

It may also be revealed by the percentage of communication that is not translated, only available in a digital format, or is not compliant with the Americans with Disabilities Act. Communicators and school leaders don't intentionally leave these groups out of their efforts, but when they fail to address these important aspects of communication, that is what happens.

It may also show us implications beyond PR efforts. If large percentages of the community population are not getting information from us, they are likely not hearing about our jobs or getting hired in our school or district.

It is important to reveal these trends not to shame people but to bring unintentional bias to the conscious level so that we can do something about it.

DEMONSTRATING VALUE

Lastly, collecting data helps us demonstrate the value of school communication and the impact on connectedness and learning. Improving school relationships and engagement is one of the most effective ways of quickly improving academic indicators as well.

When families understand a school or teacher's vision and are armed with tools to assist with learning at home, students win. When students' lives are better understood so that schools and districts can provide culturally relevant instruction and communication, we all win.

Home visit programs are a great example. When teachers get the chance to visit family homes before or during the school year, they learn a great deal about the children they are working with.

This information can inform their teaching practice, from whether or not they assign certain types of homework, to the kinds of materials they ask students to provide, to the cultural references and examples they include in the classroom.

Online parent portals are another great tool if families have access at home or at family resource centers on campus. Families can track how their child is doing in different classes, communicate electronically with the teacher, and access a wide variety of resources that allow them to supplement learning at home.

The resulting student academic data on families that utilize the portal and families that don't is likely to demonstrate the impact that the tool can have on a student's learning and success.

So while collecting data is adding a little more work and another step in the communication process, the reality is that qualifying issues with data collection will ensure that school and district staff are spending limited resources on the most important items and addressing them in the most impactful way.

KEY IDEAS IN THIS CHAPTER

- Data can help us identify and understand an issue, key audiences, and the most effective communication solutions.
- Data can help us track and evaluate our communication efforts.
- When we use data, we can stop guessing and make better decisions.
- Data also helps us to demonstrate the value of PR work and it's connection to student success.

CASE STUDY 1.1—WHAT WORKS IN ONE PLACE, DOESN'T WORK IN ANOTHER

In Nora Carr's previous district, a large urban/suburban school system that struggled with public perception issues, she developed a broad, marketing-oriented campaign that included advertising, videos, media outreach, direct mail, and printed collateral. It was very successful, and community perception rose dramatically.

Carr explains that when she made a move to Guilford County Schools, a district also suffering from negative perception issues, the same approach would have "blown up." Having just moved to the area, she did research to find out the best strategies and messages for a positive impact in her new school community.

"Research and talking to people helps keep you from stepping in it," she explains.

The new community was more skeptical of a polished campaign approach. Carr's team implemented a grassroots-oriented, community relations effort, developing several advisory councils to collect feedback on the front end and to provide ongoing input on a variety of issues.

As a result, they printed very little collateral and spent a lot of time utilizing face-to-face conversations, email, and social media.

They did some charter school competition focus group work to learn more about effective competitive messaging and trained principals, teachers, and parents to carry the message forward. According to Carr, they were "training people how to talk in a way that our parents would hear and listen." They did the "seed work" to develop trust, including one-on-one interviews, online surveys, and a listening and learning tour.

"It was a very different approach, but we achieved similar results: gains over time in interest and awareness and ultimately growth in enrollment."

Chapter Two

The Four-Step Public Relations Process

"Being busy does not always mean real work. The object of all work is production or accomplishment and to either of these ends there must be forethought, system, planning, intelligence, and honest purpose, as well as perspiration."

—Thomas A. Edison

Most television shows and movies that include a communication professional give the impression that most savvy PR people come up with brilliant campaigns at a moment's notice and based exclusively on their intuition. For example, Olivia Pope from the television show *Scandal* routinely develops an extensive crisis response in the span of an hour-long show and always looks impeccable doing it.

The real genius behind most PR campaigns is in the planning. Is it built on a foundation of accurate information, does it consider the audiences, and does it include messaging and tactics specific to those audiences?

Fortunately, there is an established four-step process that can serve as guidance in the development of an effective plan. While there are multiple variations on the names for the process, the steps are basically the same.

The two most common are RPIE and RACE. R-P-I-E lists the steps as research, planning, implementation, and evaluation. The R-A-C-E approach also starts with research and ends with evaluation, but it identifies analysis and communication as the second and third steps. Either approach, as outlined in Table 2.1, is a helpful tool in creating a thoughtful approach to public relations work.

Table 2.1.

RACE	RPIE	Step Description
	Research	• Define challenge, concern, or opportunity—one-time situation or ongoing? • Describe desired situation • Use primary, secondary, qualitative, quantitative, formal, and/or informal research • Supportive and challenging forces • Who is involved and/or affected and how? • Who is influential?
Analysis	Planning	• Audiences the program should reach and affect—don't forget internal audiences • Define specifically—demographics, psychographics, behavior toward messages/issues • What should be achieved with the public to accomplish the program goal • Four parts—audience, behavior/action, measurement, and timeframe • Changes needed to achieve the outcomes in the objectives • Message content that must be communicated to each audience to achieve the outcomes stated in the objectives • Media/channels that best reach the target publics
Communication	Implementation	• Specific tools and steps needed for each strategy—website, event, brochure, Facebook, e-news story, op-ed, etc. • Staff responsible for implementing each tactic • Sequence of events and schedule • Costs of each tactic—don't forget time, subscriptions, materials
	Evaluation	• How outcomes specified in the goals and objectives will be measured—e.g., vote, attendance, open rate, survey response, etc. • How results will be reported to management teams and used to make the program better

RESEARCH

It's no coincidence that research is the first step in almost any PR process. Understanding as much as possible about an issue, the impacted audiences, and their communication preferences is a foundational step. It is similar to the concrete slab underneath a house—if it's not solid, it's impossible to build a sturdy structure.

For example, developing a plan to improve enrollment at a middle school might include looking at the enrollment trends in the regional area and surveying families and students about what they are looking for in a school and what social media platforms they utilize.

Using that information as a starting point will ensure personalized, persuasive messaging, and effective tools and tactics are included in the next step.

PLANNING/ANALYSIS

The planning/analysis step brings together the information collected through the foundational research in the development of a comprehensive plan. The plan should address the primary audiences/stakeholders. This would include the groups of people most affected by the particular issue and potential influencers—groups or individuals that others may turn to as an authority on the topic.

Internal audiences, such as school secretaries, can serve as highly effective influencer groups on a variety of issues. They interact with classified support staff on the campus and at the district office, as well as with site teachers, students, and families.

When thinking through both primary and secondary/influencer audiences, it is important to take note of specific demographics and psychographics. For example, demographics might include language spoken, socioeconomic status, internet access, and neighborhood—basically anything that answers the question of who they are.

Psychographics provide a window into what the group thinks and why. Understanding that fifth-grade students are heavily influenced by their peers on the topic of which middle school to attend is extremely helpful psychographic information.

The plan should also include campaign objectives for each audience. What should be achieved with each in order to accomplish the campaign goal and how will it be measured? Truly measurable objectives include four parts—the audience, the behavior change, how it will be measured, and the timeframe in which the change will happen. Chapter 6 dives into the specifics of how to develop measurable objectives.

Based on the audiences and objectives, campaign strategies and tactics round out the plan. This would include the key messages, the channels that best reach each target audience, and the specific tools needed for each strategy.

The tactics section is a granular description of the action to be taken and might include a website, an event, a fact sheet, a Facebook advertisement, or another tool identified as potentially effective for the audience.

COMMUNICATION/IMPLEMENTATION

Once the plan is fleshed out, the next step is the one most visible to the outside world. The communication/implementation step is what you typically see reflected in television and movie portrayals of PR. It is where the rubber meets the road and the detailed plan is enacted—the events are held, the tweets are sent out, the media pitches are made, and the editorial is written and sent off.

While it is a distinct phase for the purposes of planning, there is still a great deal of planning, measuring, and tracking happening during this step. If the outputs—measured indicators of the tactics—are not showing the results we expect, we don't have to wait for the evaluation to change course.

Tweets not getting enough engagement? Take another look at the message—is it tailored to the audience? Is it tailored for Twitter? Pull in a few members of the intended audience and brainstorm some tweaks to the message or think about changing tactics altogether, shifting your time and energy.

EVALUATION

In many cases, communication/implementation is the end of the campaign story. For most school leaders, they are off and running to the next issue (or five) at their door. However, if we don't take the time to review our efforts, it is difficult to learn what worked and what didn't.

For example, did more people attend the event this year? How did they find out about the event? If none of the people that attend report that they heard about it through the expensive and time-consuming printed newsletter, maybe it's time to cut back on the number of issues each year or stop it altogether so there is more time and resources available for other effective communication tools.

Evaluation is dependent on two additional areas—setting measurable objectives and tracking communication tactics. In fact, it is incredibly difficult to accurately evaluate a campaign effort without them.

In Chapter 6, we'll discuss the key elements of a measurable objective and how to write one. Several other chapters can help with data sources (Chapter 4), surveys, (Chapter 5) and analytics (Chapter 8) to help with the tracking and measuring of activities.

All of these steps, from research to evaluation, play a role in the long-term success of an organization's PR efforts. Understanding of the community, school-related issues, and communication preferences will continue to grow, and the people conducting the campaigns will develop more sophistication and depth.

While the planning process may not be an exciting component of an hour-long sitcom, in real life the most successful Olivia Popes are the ones who spend a great deal of time conducting and looking at research, planning out campaigns, and evaluating how well specific tactics performed so they can be even more effective in the next campaign.

KEY IDEAS IN THIS CHAPTER

- RPIE and RACE are established four-step processes that can serve as guidance in the development of an effective plan.
- Start a campaign with the research step to understand as much as possible about an issue, the impacted audiences, and their communication preferences.
- The planning/analysis step brings together the information collected in the development of a comprehensive plan.
- The communication/implementation step is when the detailed plan is enacted and is the most visible part of a campaign.
- Evaluation is the review of our campaign efforts to learn what worked and what didn't.

CASE STUDY 2.1—ADDRESSING A BUS DRIVER DILEMMA WITH THE FOUR-STEP PROCESS

Every year it was an issue for Tuscaloosa City Schools: How were they going to get enough bus drivers for the year? They had tried a number of things, including banners on buses and newspaper ads, but they rarely got enough applicants, and those that applied didn't stick around.

Every six months they turned to Coordinator of Public Relations Lesley Bruinton for advertising help in recruiting a new group of drivers. Frustrated by the lack of evaluative data on the banners and ads, Bruinton asked the district to take a step back and do some additional research before deciding how to move forward.

She started with a simple suggestion: "In order for us to do this the right way," she said, "you have to tell me how you hired the people you actually hired. We need our current employees to tell us how they discovered the job."

She sat down with professionals in the human resources and transportation department to conduct a strengths, weaknesses, threats, and opportunities analysis of the situation. They quickly identified a huge weakness in the job opportunity—the initial outlay of money without any guarantee of a paid position.

To even be considered for the position, an applicant had to undergo a medical evaluation, obtain a commercial driving license, and take part in specialized training, all at their own cost for a position that wasn't very high-paying.

They also noted that every spring, Tuscaloosa had run a classified ad for a cost of $800 and that ad resulted in the hiring of two people, which meant the district was spending $400 on each new hire.

Armed with both of these pieces of information, the team petitioned the board to adjust the policy and to start offering an incentive package for bus drivers. After six months, drivers would be reimbursed for the cost of all of those items that were considered financial hurdles. Sometimes the best communication solutions are policy solutions.

They also teased out the strengths of the job, starting with looking at the data around who was successful at becoming a bus driver. Believing that it would be a great job for someone retired, they were surprised to find that the typical driver was a fifty-five-year-old African American woman who also had another job.

As they dug into the kind of work their drivers were doing in their other jobs through an interview with the transportation director, they found that drivers were also often hairdressers and pastors. What the other positions had in common was they didn't provide healthcare, obviously a key strength of the bus-driving position.

Using that valuable information, Bruinton produced a video with a hairdresser/bus driver about why she drives and another with a pastor who explained what a blessing it was to find the job because healthcare would be expensive for a small church, an issue many churches face.

She sent the video out to an officer in a pastor's association and asked him to share it. She also used the videos in paid ads on social media and posted it on the district website.

The campaign utilizing policy changes and audience-specific videos worked. The department was finally fully staffed and has remained at high employment levels since.

Bruinton sees the example as a reflection of a tendency in school administrators to recognize a problem and just think they need a quick public relations solution.

"Sometimes they don't understand the process behind it," she explains. "They don't always know what we need to collect in terms of data to refine our work. Rather than addressing issues in a tactical way, we have to coach school leaders to look at things in a systematic way. Getting colleagues to think about it differently, it's our role."

CASE STUDY 2.2—PR PROCESS
IS PART OF THE CULTURE

The four-step public relations process is part of the department culture at Clovis Unified, and something the entire team revisits in ongoing training.

"I've created an expectation with my staff that we make decisions based on data and plan out campaigns rather than simply execute tactics," Communications Director Kelly Avants explains.

They recently worked through two very challenging issues: changes to the majority of their school boundaries and the transition to the Common Core curriculum. In both cases, the changes brought up a lot of concern in stakeholder groups.

Avants credits the four-step process and detailed planning for keeping the team on track. Even though they experienced a great deal of incidental negativity, they stuck with the data-driven plan the team had developed.

"Our plans kept us focused when encountering volatility and emotion. We knew what we needed to communicate and how to communicate it. Without the four-step process, we would be responding versus leading the dialogue."

Chapter Three

Research, Easier than You Might Think

"Research is formalized curiosity. It is poking and prying with a purpose."

—Zora Neale Hurston

When the topic of research comes up, it seems that school leaders, especially communication professionals, seem to think the area is reserved for the folks in lab coats or statisticians in front of computer screens. The truth is, our organizations are conducting research nearly every day—we just need to take notice and document what we learn.

There are a number of research myths that get in the way of people believing they can conduct research on behalf of their district. Many people think it has to be expensive or executed by an outside company. However, there are so many examples of research that was done with very little funding aside from staff time and provided the district with a great deal of helpful information.

Another myth is that each time an issue comes up, there needs to be a new effort to conduct a unique research process. The truth is that research doesn't have to be done specifically for your topic. Many times, a district can add a question or two into an already-planned survey and get plenty of information on the subject they're researching.

While it doesn't necessarily require a lot of extra time or money, getting quality results from your research requires some creativity about how to get it and some curiosity about bias.

For example, online surveys are wonderful for collecting a lot of information quickly, but if there is a significant portion of families that do not have easy access to the internet or speak a different language, it takes some creativity to reach them and some understanding of how the results may be skewed without their unique perspectives.

To understand how to be creative with research ideas, it helps to have some basic knowledge about the types of research available. There are four general perspectives on communication research: primary/secondary, qualitative/quantitative, formal/informal, and formative/evaluative. Most research techniques can be classified using these perspectives that are outlined in Table 3.1.

Table 3.1.

Question: Who collected the information?	
Primary	**Secondary**
• Survey of your families or staff • Number of people who called about a specific concern • Interviews with subject matter experts	• State or federal data on education issues • City or neighborhood demographic information • Regional academic data
Question: Words or numbers?	
Qualitative	**Quantitative**
• Focus groups • Open-ended questions on surveys • Observing behavior	• Multiple choice, rating, or true/false questions on surveys • Counting the number of people who attend an event • Enrollment numbers at a school or in a program
Questions: Can it be replicated, and is it random?	
Formal(ish)	**Informal**
• Automated phone system survey • Online survey (as long as the entire population has access or survey is also provided in print) • Documenting positive, neutral, and negative press coverage based on pre-established protocol	• Interviews with key influencers • Focus groups to test messages or strategies • Group meetings allowing public feedback
Question: How will it be used?	
Formative	**Evaluative**
• Baseline survey of audience awareness, attitude, or behavior • Feedback on initial messaging and strategies • Documenting historical enrollment trends	• Post-campaign survey of audience awareness, attitude, or behavior • Measuring growth of enrollment after a campaign • Measuring growth in event attendance against the prior year

PRIMARY VERSUS SECONDARY

"Who collected the information?" is the most important question to ask when deciding if the research is primary or secondary. If you or your organization collected the information, the research could be classified as "primary." A survey of your families or staff, the count of the number of people who called about a specific concern, or interviews you conduct with subject matter experts would all qualify as primary research.

If someone else collected the information, that makes the research secondary, though no less useful. State- or federally-provided data on education issues, city or neighborhood demographic information, and regional academic data are all examples of helpful secondary research.

QUALITATIVE VERSUS QUANTITATIVE

This is likely the easiest category for most people to identify. When the research involves studying something that is difficult to quantify, such as first-person descriptions that are unique to the individual, it is likely qualitative. Focus groups, open-ended questions on surveys, and observing behavior at parent pick-up are all examples of qualitative research.

If you can easily quantify what you are researching, it is a different story. Multiple choice and rating or true/false questions on surveys are prime examples of quantitative research. So are other numbers-based processes such as counting how many people attend an event or looking at enrollment numbers for a school or in a program.

In short, if you want to understand the nature of something, qualitative methods can provide answers; if you want to understand the scope of an issue, that's likely quantitative territory.

FORMAL VERSUS INFORMAL

There are two essential questions related to classifying research as formal or informal: Is it random, and can it be replicated? Random means that there is an equal probability that anyone could have had a chance to participate, increasing the likelihood that the results represent a larger population. If it can be replicated and the results are very likely to turn out the same each time, that's another characteristic of formal research.

An automated phone system survey can qualify as formal research as long as the time of the call or other element doesn't unintentionally bias the results.

For example, if a live phone survey is conducted during the day, people who work are likely to be underrepresented in the results.

Online surveys can also qualify as formal as long as the entire population has internet access or if the survey is also provided in print form.

Even something that seems as subjective as documenting positive, neutral, and negative press coverage can be elevated to the level of formal research if the classification of positive, neutral, and negative is based on pre-established protocol or a set of guidelines that have been tested reliably with several classifiers who continue to come up with the same results.

Anecdotal information or feedback that is gathered by convenience is informal research. Interviews with an audience's key influencers, focus groups to test messages or strategies, or the comments gathered at group meetings allowing public feedback are all types of informal research.

While informal research results cannot be applied as representative of larger groups, informal data can be very useful supplementary information, helping to understand the exact nature of something hinted at with formal data.

FORMATIVE VERSUS EVALUATIVE

Formative and evaluative research is easy to classify based on the function the data has in a campaign. Will it help the communication planner decide what to do, or will it help the communication planner understand whether it's been done successfully?

Formative research is the kind of research that helps to discover more information about an issue or preview and test messaging or tools before they are used on a larger scale. Conducting a baseline survey of audience awareness, attitude, or behavior to benchmark where a campaign started is a great formative research tool that should be used more often.

Collecting feedback on initial messaging and strategies and documenting historical enrollment trends to predict what type of campaign will be needed are additional examples of formative research.

Evaluative research comes into play as a measurement of what a campaign has accomplished against the objectives that were set in the plan. A post-campaign survey of audience awareness, attitude, or behavior to measure growth is evaluative in nature.

Measuring the growth of student enrollment after a campaign or measuring growth in event attendance over the prior year are also evaluative research tools.

Understanding the types and examples of research available can demystify what it means to be data-driven in our approach. Once people begin to review the everyday examples of research tools that can be put to work in campaigns, the task of being well-informed about the issue and audiences and acting with intention when selecting communication methods becomes a simpler and more common approach to every communication situation.

KEY IDEAS IN THIS CHAPTER

- Organizations are conducting research nearly every day—the next step is to take notice and document what is learned.
- If you or your organization collected the information, the research can be classified as primary; otherwise, it is secondary.
- If you want to understand the nature of something, qualitative methods can provide answers; if you want to understand the scope of an issue, quantitative methods are the way to go.
- If the research methodology is random and results be replicated, it is formal; if not, it is informal (but still valuable).
- Formative research helps you decide what to do in a communication campaign; evaluative research helps you understand whether it's been done successfully.

CASE STUDY 3.1—AUDIENCE SURVEY GUIDES BUDGET CUTS

During a series of tough budget cuts a few years ago, Eudora School District had made many of the easy cuts and wanted to get community input on their budget priorities. They also hoped to provide enough information through the survey to show respondents that there are no easy answers.

They sent out a survey that described the $500,000 gap and included a list of options for cuts with the dollar amounts next to each item. For example, cuts in sports programs in the district came to a total of about $50,000, so that one item alone would not be nearly enough to help meet the challenge.

Due to the seriousness of the issue and the potential impact on schools, the survey received a lot of community responses. In addition to providing some education through the survey, the school board used feedback as a guide for cuts, and the survey results were shared with the same people who provided input with an explanation of how their participation affected the outcome.

CASE STUDY 3.2—LESS COST, MORE APPRECIATION

In Kelly Avants's district, Clovis Unified, the employee recognition event was a big deal—a dinner celebrating employees of the year that cost an average of $35,000. People seemed to enjoy the event, but it was something Avants wanted to find out more about to make sure the resources were well-spent.

"I wanted us to be more intentional, not just continue to do it in the same way because that was the way it was always done," Avants explains.

Her team pulled together some employee focus groups representing every employee type and conducted an Employee Recognition Program survey with questions like, "What makes you feel valued?"

She also collected secondary research on what other districts and Fortune 500 companies do to gather additional ideas.

As a result of all the employee input and inspired by their research, they revamped the awards program to spend less on the evening event and provided award recipients with $500 grants for something they'd want to improve at their department or site.

The response has been overwhelmingly positive, and the costs to the district are down by more than $20,000 annually.

Chapter Four

Data, Data Everywhere

"The goal is to turn data into information, and information into insight."

—Carly Fiorina

When schools and districts begin a conversation about adding research and tracking to their communication and engagement efforts, one of the first barriers is finding the time to add one more thing to an already long to-do list. The good news is that there are a number of ways to conduct research, track your efforts, and evaluate your programs without adding anything new.

Schools are notorious for conducting surveys of families and staff, usually collecting information because a pot of money is needed or a program requires data about the impact. Unfortunately, a lot of the time the surveys are being conducted by individuals or groups working in silos, which means the information doesn't get shared across departments or schools and families get inundated with requests for input and feedback.

It's easy to imagine a district where the student services department is collecting school culture information while the curriculum and instruction department is collecting information about the interventions taking place, and the budget department is tracking the specifics of how grant money was spent on after-school programs and parent training at the same school.

SURVEY LIST

Collecting a list of all the surveys that are taking place in a district is a great way to ensure that data-collection efforts are smarter and stakeholder groups don't get over-surveyed. To start, reach out to each school and district department with a request that they send a list of all survey- and communication-related tracking efforts they lead each year.

Ask about the scope of the survey, who is being surveyed, when the survey takes place, the survey format, and the contact information of the person in the school or department who is responsible for the survey or data collection. Add any additional category areas that make sense.

Next, create a centralized spreadsheet list of the district-wide survey and data collection efforts. You may begin to notice some central themes or overlap areas that can be simplified. There may also be a number of schools that are asking for the same information. Perhaps they can share survey tools, methods, and tips.

When all of the efforts are brought together in one place, it is likely easier to see that some populations in the district are given many opportunities to provide feedback and input, while others are not having their voice heard at all.

Data gives us the opportunity to dig deeper into our collection efforts. While districts may be doing a wonderful job overall, there may be some stakeholder groups that get left behind, simply as a side effect of the survey tools and methods that are being used. Internet and language accessibility are two of the more challenging barriers to getting full participation, and we'll explore strategies to address them in Chapter 5.

When all the data collection efforts are listed together, there will also be a variety of new data sources that can be applied to communication efforts. Most surveys collect information about how people receive information. Even if that wasn't a question that was asked, many times if a survey was conducted using an online tool, there are analytics that can tell a story about audience preferences.

For example, if a district sees a trend of online surveys being answered on smartphones as opposed to desktops or laptops (which is a point of data that some survey tools collect automatically), there are implications for district websites and online publications. When a large majority of stakeholders are accessing material through a mobile device, websites and online collateral should be designed mobile-first—created from a mobile perspective and expanded for other devices instead of the other way around.

That centralized list of surveys is great to have handy when an issue or decision is coming up that needs stakeholder feedback. Instead of creating a completely new survey and going through the effort of marketing that survey, review the list. Perhaps there is a survey that is going out in the immediate future to the same audiences. Simply adding a question or two to an existing survey cuts the workload for everyone involved.

HOW DID YOU HEAR?

Another easy source of data that often gets overlooked is a simple question that can be asked at every event or program registration: How did you hear about this? What's wonderful about this hack is that in addition to being very easy it also benefits from immediacy and specificity.

Usually, when we are asking people about communication preferences, they are self-reporting, meaning that they are doing their best to remember and guess at the best ways to communicate with them in general.

When you ask *as* someone is attending an event or calling to register, their recollection of how they heard about the event or program is likelier to be at the top of their mind and accurate. The results of this kind of effort will point to the communication tools that motivated participants to action, not just those that they are used to seeing on a regular basis.

For example, people may be very familiar with the weekly voicemail that their child's principal sends them each week and rate it highly as a method of communication. However, when you compare the summer school registration "How did you hear about this program?" responses, it may be that Facebook was the communication method that actually broke through the noise of all the messages parents receive and motivated them to act and sign their child up for summer school.

RECEPTION LAB

Another simple data collection idea that can help districts and schools clarify issues is to turn the reception desk into a research lab. Imagine a board member calls with upsetting news. Everyone in town is alarmed about the change from blue to white for the football uniforms, and the district needs to do something about it right away.

While it is important to give every concern serious consideration, sometimes a small group of individuals can inflate an issue into something larger simply by calling the right people.

To collect more information about the true impact of an issue, ask frontline staff to keep track of the number of times they are contacted by phone, in person, or by email about the issue.

This means keeping a notepad at their desk for a few days to a week and keeping a log of activity. Those numbers can be added to any social media engagement on the topic to come up with a clearer idea of how widespread the outrage might be.

BORROW FROM NEIGHBORS

Borrowing research from other area agencies and businesses is another data source solution that many may not have thought about. Secondary research, as it is referred to, can contain extremely helpful information that can save schools and districts time and money.

A regional government agency is likely attempting to communicate with many of the same stakeholders, and if they have already collected information about information preferences and trusted sources, their data can easily be utilized for a district outreach plan.

If district staff develop strong connections with organizations that are reaching out to the same audiences, the same kind of centralized research list could be developed to add even more data sources and opportunities for district efforts.

Imagine needing to ask a stakeholder group about internet access or bus ridership and being able to reach out to the local water district and add such a question to their survey going out the following week.

In preparation of an effective communication effort, adding a few simple, systemic changes can add a wealth of data for research and tracking and measuring activities. Easy things such as a centralized list of surveys, always asking about how audiences heard about something, and borrowing from other agencies will provide easily accessible information that you can put to use to make your communication efforts smarter and more effective.

Research doesn't have to be complicated. Table 4.1 provides additional samples of things you may already have done, but perhaps didn't call research.

KEY IDEAS IN THIS CHAPTER

- Collecting a list of all the surveys that are taking place in a district is a great way to ensure that data-collection efforts are smarter.
- Another easy source of data that often gets overlooked is a simple question that can be asked at every event or program registration: How did you hear about this?
- Clarify issues by tracking the number of contacts about it at your reception desk.
- Borrowing research from other agencies and businesses can provide a good data source.

Data, Data Everywhere 29

Table 4.1.

Source	Data
Town hall meeting	Number of participants, number of comments, pro/con/neutral rating of comments, qualitative input
Referendum results	Voter participation rates, pockets of support/non-support, voter demographics
Enrollment	Geographic mapping of student addresses, numbers up or down over previous years, comparisons to other schools/districts, demographic snapshot of current families, demographic trends
Social media engagement	Likes, comments, retweets, followers gained/lost
Transfer form	Reason for transfer (open field or multiple choice), neighborhood (from address), home school, transfer school
Parent-teacher conferences	Live survey responses; attendance rates by school, grade, and demographics
Media monitoring	Number of releases or announcements picked up, positive versus negative or neutral coverage type, success rates with various outlets, ratio of stories sent to published/aired
Surprise shopper	Data on pre-determined rubric instrument, additional observations not captured by rubric
Census	Number of families, number of children under eighteen, demographics
District app downloads	Number of downloads by school or by grade
Interview with leader or influencer	Information on topic, additional leaders or influencers to talk to, communication tool ideas
Chamber of Commerce perception survey	Awareness of programs, perception/satisfaction with schools, suggestions for programs and communication tools
Internal communication and morale survey	Ratings of communication and morale, survey participation rates by role, location

CASE STUDY 4.1—DATA DRIVES ADVERTISING

Clovis Unified School District communication staff never has to wonder where they should spend their precious advertising dollars. Each year, the district conducts a number of satisfaction surveys with parents, employees, and students. It always includes some questions about how they get their information about the district and where they get their news in general.

They also conduct surveys with non-parent groups, which make up a significant percentage of the community.

The team pays attention to web analytics, messaging system statistics, assessment office information, focus groups, and community meeting comments at the district and school-site level.

"Each year, we review all of the data. The information we discover, along with our budget and potential reach of different channels, guides our advertising buys, social media platforms, and where we spend our staff time and energy," Communications Director Kelly Avants explains.

It's an approach that ensures the district communication messages are hitting the right notes and adding new channels to their toolkit as stakeholder groups are adopting them.

Chapter Five

Designing Surveys that Truly Listen

"When we listen with curiosity, we don't listen with the intent to reply. We listen for what's behind the words."

—Roy T. Bennett

The elephant in the room when it comes to surveys is this: don't ask if you don't plan to do anything with the results. Surveys are work for everyone involved. They have to be designed, written, put into the correct platform, tested, revised, distributed, and marketed.

The results have to be tallied, analyzed, and interpreted for action—and that's just on the organization side. Respondents invest time taking the survey as well. Before anyone decides to conduct a survey, they must first decide if they *really* want input.

If the results come back and they don't align with the expectation or direction the organization was planning to take, what will happen? Is this a sincere effort to collect guidance and feedback from stakeholders or a show of engagement to check a box or appease a certain group?

The worst thing an organization can do is ask for opinions and not use them. Respect the time of everyone involved and only use a survey if the feedback will matter.

QUESTIONS TO ASK BEFORE YOU SURVEY

After the biggest question is out of the way, there are a few more that will help shape the development of a survey. What's the purpose of the survey? What is the organization trying to learn or understand?

Is it a survey to tease out overall perceptions of the organization, determine support for a program, or discover communication preferences? Will it help establish a baseline so that a change in perception, awareness, or self-reported behavior can be measured following a campaign?

Next, what will a parent, student, or community member get from completing the survey? What's their stake in helping the school or district? This important question will help guide the marketing of the survey.

Is there a way to tie the benefit of the survey back to students and families? The results will guide decision-making on an issue, provide insight about the features wanted in a new school or program, or help the school or district better communicate, strengthening families' capacity to support student learning.

When and how are respondents likely to engage in the survey and what devices, if any, are they likely to use? Popular survey methodologies include online (via a computer, tablet, or smartphone to a survey portal), telephone (via automated dialing responses to a voice prompt or speaking with a live surveyor), and in-person responding to questions from a live surveyor.

Analytics of previous surveys, if available, can provide insights into preferred options. If the data shows a significant population lacks access to the internet, maybe an online survey is not the best tool for the job.

If English is a second language for a significant segment of the population being surveyed, ensuring the survey is available in other languages is essential. It goes without saying—available resources, including funds for the required technology or live surveyors, will need to be factored into the decision.

Lastly, when is the last time that a survey was sent out to the same audience? If you've created a centralized list of surveys as described in Chapter 2, you'll have that information at your fingertips. It's important to not over-survey your stakeholders.

Reserve the request for the times you truly need input to make a good decision or plan to move forward. Consider if a full survey is needed or questions can be added to one that is already scheduled.

It's also important to find as "neutral" a time as possible—for example, not when teachers are pressured at the end of quarters or semesters to get grades in, not when it's standardized testing time, not when there are lots of other activities that involve parents, such as start of school or end of school year, and so on. Be prepared to move your survey if a crisis hits.

SURVEY DESIGN AND DEVELOPMENT

Once the decisions around purpose, methodology, and schedule are determined, it is time to outline the survey. Based on the type of feedback the organization needs to collect through the effort, develop an outline with a general phrase to represent each question or section of questions while not worrying about the specific wording yet.

The outline helps with ordering the questions in a way that makes sense for the respondents. For example, group questions about a similar topic together, and start with foundational or general questions before moving to more specific questions.

When the outline is complete, it is time to craft the wording. In the introduction, aim to be transparent with the audience about the purpose of the study, including language in marketing messages. The purpose might include how the input will be used and what changes are likely to be made from the feedback.

When possible, tie the effort back to how it will impact students and student learning. If the survey is anonymous, let respondents know so up front. Anonymous surveys are more likely to receive honest critical feedback if respondents are confident that they won't be identified through their answers.

After the introduction and overview, consider the demographic information you wish to collect on the respondents. Knowing how you will want to analyze the results by different segments of your survey population will help guide these decisions.

Will you want to know the respondent's connection to the school or district? Another might be the length of relationship with the school or district, or how they heard about the survey. Table 5.1 is an example of the categories to consider including in a question about respondent's role in the district.

The more categories that are included, the more specific the analysis of the data can be. For example, using cross tabulation, usually an easy automatic function of most online survey tools, the responses to questions on the rest of the survey can be separated by the answer to the role question. How district administrators answered a question can be compared to how teachers answered the same question.

Table 5.1.

Please select the option below that best represents your role with ABC School District.

- A) Parent or family member of a student
- B) Student
- C) Community member; not a parent or staff member
- D) Teacher
- E) Site support
- F) Site administrator
- G) District support
- H) District administrator

One note of caution on demographic questions: if the survey is anonymous, give consideration to questions that may compromise that anonymity. For example, if you ask respondents to identify the school where they work and also ask them to identify their job title, a principal, school secretary, or music teacher is most likely the only one in that role, making their answers easy to connect back to them as individuals.

Throughout the development of the survey, pay special attention to the specific wording. Keep the language as simple as possible, creating a conversational tone and avoiding educational jargon. If the survey is being written in Microsoft Word, one of the proofing options is to show readability statistics. The same option is available in Google Docs. The readability score will provide an initial idea of how accessible the survey will be for respondents.

Cultural considerations are also important when it comes to wording. For example, one change that has been made in a lot of schools and districts is the reference to the adult responsible for a student. In the past, that word has usually been "parent."

However, a number of social and demographic changes have increased the number of households in which someone other than a parent is the adult that schools and districts are communicating with. Instead, many schools and districts are now using the terms "families" or "family member" to ensure all households are represented.

In addition to wording, questions with rating scales should remain consistent throughout the survey, and it is generally helpful to have the lowest mark on the left and the highest on the right, although the research on the topic doesn't indicate an impact on results.

Table 5.2 provides an example of a question with a Likert scale response that meets these guidelines.

If it is a multiple-choice question, be sure that all the possible response categories are offered or include "other" as an option so that every respondent sees an answer that reflects their experience.

In addition to the wording and the format of each individual question, the length of the survey needs to be considered. How long will it take to com-

Table 5.2.

Please rate your agreement with the following statements on a scale of 1 to 5.
1 (Strongly disagree)   2(Disagree)   3(Neutral)   4(Agree)   5(Strongly agree)

My child's school is a welcoming place for parents.	1	2	3	4	5
My child's teacher appreciates parent volunteers in the classroom.	1	2	3	4	5
I feel like my opinion is valued by my child's school staff.	1	2	3	4	5

plete? As a general rule, five minutes or less is recommended. On occasion, a longer survey might be needed.

In either case, it's a good idea to let the respondents know how long they should expect to spend on the survey. A "progress bar" at the top of each page also helps them gauge the experience.

Once the initial draft is complete, select the most appropriate survey tool and send a test version out to a small sample of respondents. Talk with the sample respondents about the purpose of each question and whether they interpreted them consistently and in the way they were intended. Rework questions that are confusing for respondents.

When the survey has been pretested and the wording is finalized, it's time to send it out. If it is a survey by invitation, it should be sent to a representative sample of the full audience universe. With a sample, you need to get a much higher percentage of people responding than when going with the full universe to get the same margin of error.

Like any other communication effort, develop a plan for how to reach potential respondents. If it is an internal survey for employees, the outreach

Table 5.3.

Audience	Activity	Timeline	Completed
Students	Announce launch and close in government class		
Parents	District site website link		
Parents	Send launch and close via text		
Parents	Phone message about launch and close		
Parents	Include in school newsletters		
Parents	Include on school websites—launch		
Parents	Provide paper copies in school offices for families without internet		
Parents	Provide paper copies in backpacks for rural schools		
Parents, staff, community	Post launch in district newsletter		
Parents, community	Post launch/close to district Facebook		
Parents, community	Post launch/close to community Facebook pages		
Community	Send blurb and link to community groups for sharing via email lists, newsletters, etc.		
Community	District Twitter accounts post survey launch/close		
Staff	Send link via email at open and close		

Survey Outreach Plan

is simple and can be accomplished through email invitations and department announcements.

If a school or district has email addresses for all families, a similar approach may work. If not, the school or district should review the audiences that need to be reached and the communication tools available, developing a plan for getting the survey invitation out as many ways as possible. Table 5.3 is an example of a survey outreach plan.

SURVEY DISTRIBUTION

In general, two weeks is a good period of time to leave a survey open. Any longer than that and people may feel they have plenty of time to respond and forget. Shorter than that may not leave enough time for maximum responses.

Try to avoid holidays or breaks as part of the two-week period if possible. Keep in mind, though, that an extension of the survey period that does not present conflict could result in a higher response rate and may be worthwhile to the cause.

The outreach plan should include an initial invitation and at least one reminder on the day before the survey ends. Depending on the audience and the number of communication tools, a midpoint reminder might be a good option, but if there are multiple tools being utilized, it could be over the top.

Some districts have found multiple reminders to yield good results, so it is a decision that will be based on your unique circumstances and audiences. In either case, the reminders can and should be delivered in different ways and at different times of the day and week to minimize any bias that can occur with who is receiving the messages.

While outreach is important, it's the content that drives participation rates in Peel District School Board surveys. In a recent mental health survey of staff, they realized a 90 percent response rate.

Carla Pereira, director of communications for the Canadian district, explains that anything that helps staff impact students in a positive way or that helps them monitor student achievement and well-being is always a top interest area. In the outreach plan, it should be easy to communicate how the survey will benefit students.

Once the overall outreach plan is developed, think through the survey outreach messaging as thoroughly as the survey wording. Keep it short, conversational, and use simple wording.

Remember to include the language around the purpose for the survey and how the information will support students and student learning. It may be helpful to add a sample question that is easy to answer.

For example, in a survey about communication preferences, try something such as: "How are you reading this? We want to know! Help ABC School get even better at communicating with our families!" Develop tool-specific messages that are longer for media articles and websites and shorter for Facebook and Twitter. Given the right amount of time and effective messaging, the responses should roll in.

VOLUNTARY BIAS

When a survey is open to any respondent to opt in, be mindful of the potential for voluntary response bias. This occurs when results are comprised largely of respondents having strong opinions on one side or another of an issue.

The resulting responses tend to overrepresent people who have strong opinions on one side or another of an issue. There may not be anything that can be done to avoid this kind of bias; it just needs to be accounted for when interpreting the results.

For example, on a survey of changing school start times, families may be polarized into two camps: very much in support of the change or very against the change. When compared to the total number of possible respondents, however, it becomes obvious the vast majority doesn't have an opinion on the topic that is strong enough to motivate them to take the survey. Attaining a large percentage of respondents translates to a low margin of error and can help overcome voluntary response bias.

SURVEY INCENTIVES

Incentives offer another area of consideration. Contests in which responses are entered for prizes can sometimes increase the number of people who participate in a survey but may compromise the quality of responses. If people technically are able to submit multiple responses to win a prize, it may taint the representativeness of the population as a whole.

Lastly, the survey responses need to be reviewed not just for the content, but also for representation in significant segments of the survey population. If a particular segment is not participating, do some digging to find out why.

Did they not hear about the survey through the communication tools that were used? Did they feel that their voice wouldn't be heard and they didn't want to waste their time? A small focus group may lead to some great insights about gaps in trust or communication methods.

FINAL STEPS

Analysis and interpretation may seem like the final steps with a survey, but there are three more: What will change as a result of the input? What decisions will be affected? How will the information guide future programs and communication efforts?

These questions need to be both asked and answered. The "so what" of the results needs to be identified and translated into a focused explanation of what was learned. "Here is what we learned, and here is what we plan to do about it." The "so what" can then be utilized as post-messaging for the survey and turned into visuals and graphics that make it easy to understand what the results mean. There is a lot more discussion of the reporting of data in Chapter 9 of this book.

Lastly, in addition to telling audiences what you learned, do not forget to thank them for their time and input. Use the same outreach plan you used with your participation campaign to let them know that you listened and the time they spent on the survey is valued.

List the numbers that participated, key insights, and how those insights will be applied to make the organization better at serving students and families. This may impact both the likelihood that they will participate the next time as well as their respect and support for the organization.

We all like to be heard, even when a decision doesn't go our way. At the very least, we like to know the time and energy we invested in something mattered. Table 5.4 provides a list of tips for creating, formatting, and distributing a survey.

It may all seem overwhelming at first, especially if the organization is new to asking for guidance and feedback. The most important thing is to keep asking. You may not learn all that you expect to with your first survey, but you will learn something, even if it is how to do better with the next one.

KEY IDEAS IN THIS CHAPTER

- Only use a survey if the feedback will impact the issue. If the decision has already been made, don't make the mistake of asking for input.
- Think through the format, timing, organization, and wording of the survey to ensure it is effective.
- Pretest the survey with representatives of the target audience when possible.
- Use a communication plan to increase survey participation and communicate the results after the survey.

Table 5.4.

Top 20 List of General Survey Tips

1. Don't ask if the results won't change anything.
2. Know your purpose and communicate it to the respondents.
3. Know what's in it for respondents and communicate it.
4. Design the survey for the way it will be taken—desktop, laptop, phone, paper, verbal.
5. Don't over survey; use information from other efforts when possible.
6. Create an outline before you attempt question wording.
7. Order survey questions by topic area.
8. If you say the survey will be anonymous, ensure it will be.
9. Use simple language in descriptive text and questions; avoid educational jargon.
10. Consider cultural differences in terms of the wording and distribution.
11. Rating scales should be consistent.
12. Keep the survey to less than five minutes.
13. Pretest and revise.
14. Let respondents know how long it will take and where they are in the survey.
15. Create a communication plan for the survey distribution.
16. Keep it open for about two weeks, avoiding holidays and breaks.
17. Be thoughtful in creating survey outreach messaging.
18. Consider possible bias impacts in analyzing results.
19. Clearly define and articulate the "so what" of the results.
20. Reuse your outreach plan to tell people you listened and what will change.

CASE STUDY 5.1—SURVEY QUESTIONS

There are three questions Nicole Kirby, director of communication services at Park Hill School District, pays close attention to in ongoing annual surveys. The first two relate to "efforts of the district to communicate" and "efforts to involve citizens in decision-making," and she has been watching those numbers for more than ten years, adjusting the communication team efforts and conducting additional research when needed to discover the reasons behind survey results going up or down in a given area.

The third question asks people how they get information about the district. There have been a lot of changes in the responses to this question over time, directly guiding the district's tactics. Today, Park Hill spends less time on media releases and more on tactics related to opinion leaders and key communicators because families are turning more and more to friends and neighbors.

Chapter Six

What Gets Measured Gets Done
Creating Accountability

"A goal properly set is halfway reached."

—Zig Ziglar

Even when people are determined to follow the four-step process, conduct foundational research, track their efforts, and evaluate their success, there seems to be a stumbling block when it comes to developing truly measurable objectives for a communication campaign.

Perhaps it is the fear that they won't meet the objective that drives the reluctance to document the desired outcome. Developing a culture that accepts that objectives won't always be met and that sometimes we learn more when they are not is key.

Three main elements make up a truly measurable objective: it must be time-bound, audience-specific, and document a measurable phenomenon (action, perception, awareness, etc.). There are a couple of exceptions to the rule that will be discussed later in the chapter, but for the most part, those three elements should be a part of each one.

TIME-BOUND

If an objective is not made time-bound, then there is always a possibility that it could happen at some point—the effort could simply continue into infinity. You can never fail at an objective without an associated time period.

To set one, think through the amount of time it will take to have the intended impact on the specific audience. Look at how long it has taken other schools or districts to do the same thing if that data is available. If that doesn't provide any guidance, you can always take a general approach with an annual measurement.

The central question that must be answered is, "When will it happen?" The answer depends on the effort and may be a month and year, an event date, or even a survey date. For example, enrollment to rise a certain amount by the state attendance audit date or for perception to go up by an annual communication and culture survey in May.

There is no wrong answer to this question; it is just a matter of committing to look for a change at a certain time.

AUDIENCE-SPECIFIC

The first step to making your objective audience-specific is to narrow down to your key audiences. That doesn't mean your messages and strategies won't impact other audiences, it just means that as a result of conducting and analyzing the data, the audiences that will be the most helpful in the campaign are identified as "key."

There are two factors to consider when narrowing to key audiences: what is the group that will be the most impacted by the issue?; and what is the group that is the most influential with the impacted group?

In addition to developing measurable objectives, identifying key audiences is very helpful for messaging. The more specific the message, the more likely it will speak to the intended audience—their hopes, aspirations, challenges, beliefs, and perceptions. General messages are not nearly as impactful as those designed with an audience in mind.

Key audiences might be fifth- through seventh-grade families if the district is working on future changes to graduation requirements and the seventh graders will be the first affected class.

A key audience might also be a group unrelated to the school. For example, a campaign in the Los Angeles area discovered that a group of folk dance teachers were highly influential with mothers in the area, well-regarded and respected. They had no formal association with the organization, which made them a key audience to include in activities, messaging, and measuring.

One of the most important reasons to narrow down to key audiences in a communication effort is to measure. If a campaign's messages and strategies are designed to impact a particular group, and as a result of checking in with that specific audience through a survey or through observable behavior, you learn that campaign is falling short, it can be adjusted.

If the focus of the campaign is too broad, the strategies may not be working with the most impactful audience groups, but that failure can be hidden by the positive response of other groups.

MEASURABLE ACTION

Selecting and focusing on the action is the last step in the objective development process. There are three questions to ask in deciding on the action that will be measured. What change do you want to see regarding behavior, perception, knowledge, support, or something else?

Secondly, how much change do you want to see? In most cases, this looks like a percentage increase or a number increase over where things are before the campaign starts.

Lastly, the piece that is sometimes missing is how exactly to measure it. If there is no way to measure something, it is impossible to include it in a measurable objective.

Many behaviors (observed and self-reported) can be included in a measurable objective. An increase in enrollment, an increase in positive perception, a decrease in truancy, or an increase in support are all examples of the typical behavior changes included in a school communication plan.

The amount of change gets a little trickier. For example, it could be a 10 percent increase, fifty more participants in an event, or twenty-five new students in a school. It is hard to know how challenging to make the objective.

Looking back at trend lines in a certain area can be very helpful. If a school has been steadily losing ten students a year, perhaps a healthy objective is to shoot for stabilizing enrollment and not losing a student in the coming year.

If a school or district hasn't been tracking the area that is to be measured, it can help to look at examples in other similar-sized districts. Typically, the National School Public Relations Association (NSPRA) or a state-sponsored chapter of the NSPRA can help with identifying other districts that have conducted similar campaigns.

How to measure the change is the last part of the behavior piece. Measurements can include self-reported information about awareness, perception, and support gathered in pre-campaign and post-campaign surveys about the behavior, attendance tracking at events, enrollment tracking at schools, or even a vote tally in an election.

It can be tempting to include social media analytics in this area. If the objective is to gain followers so that they have access to information that supports student learning, a case can be made to use an increase in followers as a measurable objective. However, unless the measurable behavior is tied to an action that supports student learning, it may simply be an output or tool used to keep the campaign on track.

Measurable objectives are incredibly useful not only for measuring a campaign's success but also for providing clarity and focus during the campaign. In the course of developing and implementing a communication campaign, it is part of the process to come up with a wide variety of strategies and tactics

Table 6.1.

Objective Question	Examples
Who do you hope to impact with your efforts?	Students, families, teachers, staff, community members
What change do you want to see—behavior, perception, knowledge, support?	Increased enrollment, increase in positive perception, decrease in truancy, increase in support
How much change do you want to see?	10 percent increase or decrease, 50 more participants, 25 new students
How exactly will you measure it?	Pre-/post-surveys, enrollment audit day, attendance data
By when will it happen?	Month and year, event date, survey date

and only a subset of the ideas created may be viable due to the budget, staffing, or time available.

Clearly-defined measurable objectives provide a helpful filter. Which strategies and tactics are likely to meet the objective? While all of the strategies may be interesting, some of them will better meet the objective. Table 6.1 provides the main questions to consider in developing a truly measurable objective and measurement ideas related to each.

EXCEPTIONS TO THE RULE

There will be times when it seems impossible to create a truly measurable objective for a campaign. One of the most frequent reasons is that the school or district has never measured that behavior before, so it is impossible to set a percent or whole number increase or decrease.

If that is the case, the objective could be to create a baseline for measuring the behavior. For example, in a district that has never asked stakeholders about their communication preferences, the objective might be to survey this year to create a baseline rating for each communication tool and to annually survey stakeholder groups to track changes in preferences the future.

In other cases, it may be impossible to measure due to lack of resources. For example, if the campaign is done in a hurry to achieve something time-bound and there is no time for a pre-survey or if the district is lacking the funds, expertise, or political will to accurately measure the behavior.

While not ideal, sometimes campaigns will need to be measured by outputs rather than the impact on behavior. For example, if a district doesn't have the time or money to do the pre- and post-survey or if there have already been several surveys that year, some outputs like social media analytics, positive media coverage, or the number of emails opened could serve as viable options.

Communication Services Balanced Scorecard

Process	Measure	Current	Stretch Goal	Above Target	Target	Below Target	Way Behind
Stakeholder Engagement	Phone survey – efforts of the district to include public in decision making	3.96	4.43	4.20	3.75	3.53	3.30
	Percentage of target number of communications that included information about community input into decisions	110.8 percent for May	150 percent	125 percent	100 percent	75 percent	50 percent
Communication	Accuracy log	One error in May	No errors in a semester	No errors in two months	No errors in a month	One error in a month	Two errors in a month
	Open rate: Insider	56.99 percent In May	70 percent	65 percent	60 percent	55 percent	50 percent
	Open rate: First Hand	30.88 percent in May	40 percent	37.5 percent	35 percent	32.5 percent	30 percent
	Phone survey – efforts of the district to communicate with patrons	4.05	4.3	4.18	4.05	3.93	3.79
	Number of communication plans	10 plans through May	16 plans per year	14 plans per year	12 plans per year	10 plans per year	8 plans per year
	Deadlines	98 percent in May	100 percent per month	99 percent per month	98 percent per month	97 percent per month	96 percent per month
	Stakeholders information needs log – percentage of target	165.7 percent for May	120 percent per month	110 percent per month	100 percent per month	90 percent per month	80 percent per month
	Facebook average monthly organic post reach	6,381 in May	5,500	5,250	5,000	4,750	4,500
	Communication about long-range facilities plan – percentage of target		150 percent	125 percent	100 percent	75 percent	50 percent

Park Hill School District
Building Successful Futures • Each Student • Every Day

Figure 6.1. Example of the data objectives Park Hill School District uses to track and measure communication activities

Outputs are also important reflections of effort. Even when a campaign misses the mark, there is still a great deal of work involved in the effort. Outputs help to tell the story of the amount of work what was involved. Figure 6.1 is an example of a set of indicators a school district is using to track their department success.

WHAT HAPPENS IF WE FAIL?

If a measured objective is set correctly, it is aspirational and is something to work toward. That means that there will be times that a campaign doesn't quite hit the mark.

That's when the best learning happens. When a campaign is successful, there is rarely a discussion about what didn't go well. When the overall objectives are met, there is (maybe) a brief celebration and then movement on to the next communication challenge or opportunity.

When a campaign doesn't hit the mark, there is a natural tendency to find out why. Whether it is professional curiosity, a desire to get better, or simply to provide an explanation to leadership, there is a much greater effort to dig into the details.

Perhaps it was the messaging: Did it fall short in communicating the benefits? Maybe it was a particular tool that wasn't appropriate for a specific audience. Output measures, such as open rates and clicks on links, can tell an important story about both.

Pulling together a debriefing group of the key audiences can also provide invaluable information as long as the questions are open-ended enough for them to explain why they think people didn't respond to the campaign in the way it was hoped.

EXAMPLES

It can be helpful to see some examples of objectives that are truly measurable as well as some that just sound that way. Let's start with the latter:

"Improve perception of ABC Middle School." While this seems like a worthwhile goal, it is impossible to measure this behavior. Does everyone's perception of ABC Middle School matter, or are there key audiences that influence decisions around enrollment?

Naming the audiences is an important element of a measurable objective. What about the timeline? If there is no set time, then the objective can never be measured. How much should the perception improve? Is one person's opinion improving a worthy target for the expenditure of taxpayer funds and staff time that a campaign will require?

A better way to write the objective in a way that is measurable might be, "Improve fifth- and sixth-grade family member perceptions of ABC Middle School by 5 percent, as measured by the annual satisfaction survey in May 2018." There is a clear definition of the audience, time period, and action that will be measured.

How about this one: "Increase attendance at XYZ High School." This is trickier because it could be argued that technically there is an implied audience as students are the ones that enroll.

There is also somewhat of an implied measurement of action because if even one more student enrolls at XYZ High School, the objective is met. However, there is no time limit so the campaign could continue indefinitely, hoping for that one student to enroll.

A more defined and reasonable objective would read, "Increase attendance by 20 percent at XYZ High School prior to October 2019." The audience is still implied, but the action increase and timeline are explicit. In October 2019, there will be a definitive answer about whether or not this objective was met.

KEY IDEAS IN THIS CHAPTER

- There are three critical elements of a measurable objective—time-bound, audience-specific, and measurable action, perception, or awareness.
- If the school or district has never measured that behavior before, then the objective could be to create a baseline for measuring the behavior.
- While not ideal, sometimes campaigns will need to be measured by outputs rather than the impact on behavior.
- The best learning happens when a campaign doesn't meet objectives.

CASE STUDY 6.1—WALL OF DATA

The data wall in the Communication Services Department at Park Hill School District is a comprehensive reflection of the department's work with stakeholder groups. Using a variety of tracking and research tools, including surveys, audits, and analytics, they track nearly everything related to communication.

Using content audits to gather the data, the wall includes the percentage of communication that included information about community input into decisions and about the district's long-range facilities plan.

It also includes an accuracy log that tracks errors in department materials, open rates on e-newsletters, and phone survey statistics including respondents' ratings of the efforts of the district to include the public in decision-making and the efforts of the district to communicate with patrons.

It even includes data on everyday outputs from the department such as the number of communication plans and deadlines met. Figure 6.1 is an example of the outputs collected.

The department staff sets goals for themselves in each category and continually tracks where they currently are against them, from "way behind" to "target" to "stretch goal." It's a valuable tool for the team to keep their performance goals visible as it is always posted on a department wall.

One unintended consequence has been the effect on other senior leaders in the district when they see the wall. According to Director of Communication Services Nicole Kirby, the typical response is, "I didn't realize you were doing all this!"

Chapter Seven

Analytics, the Low-Hanging Data Fruit

"Numbers have an important story to tell, they rely on you to give them a clear and convincing voice"

—Stephen Few

One of the wonderful things about doing public relations work today is the amount of data easily available through analytics. It may be hard to imagine a world not that long ago in which practitioners had to guess at what the audience was responding to or conduct expensive and time-consuming surveys to get the same information that today is available with a simple click.

The challenge is to weed through all of the data now available to get to the numbers that mean the most to your communication efforts.

It can be very tempting to dive down the data hole, get lost in reviewing the statistics, and wonder about the stories they are telling—and that is not a bad thing to do once in a while to ensure you are not missing anything.

One helpful approach to analytics is to identify the key metrics that impact public relations efforts and review them on a regular basis. These metrics will likely point to who is engaging with your school or district (and who is not), how and when are they engaging, and the type of content they find most engaging. Table 7.1 provides a list of the types of data that can be reviewed for each of these questions.

There are accessible analytics related to websites, social media platforms and tools, e-newsletters, automated call and text systems, online survey tools, and parent portals. While the variety of data available through program analytics is staggering, for the purpose of this book, we'll cover the top three: websites, social media, and e-newsletters.

Table 7.1.

Channel or Tool	Question	Data Examples
Website	Who	Audience, new users, active users
	How	Browser, device, social referral
	Content	Page views, session duration, user flow
Social	Who	Followers, likes, unlikes, reach, fans
	How	Browser, device, top sources
	Content	Reach, clicks, reactions, comments, shares, impressions, visits, mentions, activity
E-newsletter	Who	Deliveries, clicks, open rate, unsubscribed
	How	Browser, device
	Content	Open rate, click rate, distribution, forwards
Survey	Who	Respondents
	How	Browser, device
	Content	Skipped questions, response rate, completion, visits, time to complete

WEBSITES

If your school or district is contracted with an outside company to provide websites, it is likely that the company has their own analytic tools with data that can be shared by asking. Even if a school or district website is custom or internally developed, it is very easy to add measurement tools.

Google Analytics, for example, is free and easy to set up by adding some code to your website. Once installed, Google tracks when your site is visited, demographics of your visitors, and how they found your page.

Some of the most helpful features or views include User Flow, Site Content, Dashboard, and Mobile Tool. User Flow allows you to see where users started on a site, the pages they visited, and the last page they saw before they left.

This data provides rich information about key content areas. For example, if the User Flow shows that many people are coming to your site from a page other than the homepage, what is the content that is drawing them in? And how can it be featured more prominently?

Site content analytics are a great compliment to the User Flow because this data will help identify the most popular pages and make that content easily accessible from the main pages of your website and within the navigation.

If a significant number of people are moving from the homepage to specific content elsewhere on your site, consider adding that page to a "Quick Links" section, for example. Your goal, after all, is to make your site as friendly and intuitive as possible so that your visitors find the information they are looking for as quickly as possible.

Steve Williams, cofounder and director of marketing for Campus Suite, explains the website experience: "It's not a visit to the amusement park where people are just enjoying exploring everything. It is more like a trip to the grocery store to find specific items and get out as fast as you can."

The Google Analytics Dashboard tool can also be very helpful when set up to reflect your goals and priorities. One of the first items to set is the date range because it is difficult to make assessments about content with short time periods.

Unless you are reviewing analytics for a specific event—for example, examining web traffic following a crisis event in your district—set a range of at least a month to have a reasonable portion of data to review. You can provide a unique name for the dashboard and track new users, number of sessions, and browsers utilized.

You can even set up "goals" and measure conversions, or completion rates, for each goal you set up. If Google Analytics has been on the site for a significant period of time, the Dashboard can also help you see and understand trends, comparing previous timeframes to determine improvement.

The Mobile Tool helps you determine what devices your website visitors are using, which has become increasingly important to understand. Whether audiences are experiencing your content on a desktop, on a tablet, or with a smartphone, each device works with websites in distinct ways.

For example, if you have a high number of mobile users, you should ensure that your website has a responsive design or even design for a mobile-first view. This data has implications well beyond website design, however, including your approach to creating and organizing content to be easily accessed on the devices your users are most likely using.

While all of these analytics can be helpful and informative, they can also no doubt be a little overwhelming at first. The good news is these tools are useful and accessible for virtually anyone—there is no need for advanced skillsets.

Google also offers a free online "Analytics Academy" with a course called "Google Analytics for Beginners." Starting with just a few tools and making time for a little bit of free online training will ensure you get started in the right direction.

SOCIAL MEDIA

Social media is a powerful tool that is changing the way school communities work, offering a new model to engage with families, staff, students, and the world at large. A Pew Research Center survey conducted in the spring of 2016 found that Facebook continues to be the country's most popular social networking platform.

Nearly eight in ten (79 percent) adults now use Facebook, more than double the share that uses Twitter (24 percent), Pinterest (31 percent), Instagram (32 percent), or LinkedIn (29 percent). When you account for Americans who do not use the internet at all, that means that 68 percent of all US adults are Facebook users, while 28 percent use Instagram, 26 percent use Pinterest, 25 percent use LinkedIn, and 21 percent use Twitter.

While the national statics are a gauge of overall use, a school or district's preferences are far more important when it comes to building an effective public relations campaign. When managed strategically, social media conversations help build stronger, more trusting relationships and allow school leaders to have a voice in important discussions related to the work they are doing.

If it's not already being measured, it is a good idea to add a question about social media usage to annual school district surveys. This will help school leaders stay current on family preferences—the content your stakeholders want, and where they want to receive it.

Once the school or district identifies the most important social media platforms, setting up the right analytics can assist in ensuring that important audiences are being reached. The key analytics vary by the social media platform.

For example, with Facebook, administrators will want to keep an eye on reactions, comments, and shares for each post. Digging deeper, Facebook insights can provide an overview of page activity over a given period of time as well as information on followers, reach, and the demographics of the people who like the school or district Facebook page.

One of the most valuable analytics available simply shows what day of the week and/or time of day your followers are most likely to be on Facebook—perhaps the most strategic nugget of data available when you are trying to decide the timing of your content.

At the post level, the positive reactions, comments, and shares provide good information about the kind of content that page followers want to see. While there may be other types of content that must be shared (operational and safety messages), the positively-rated posts can provide examples of the type of content the school or district should post more often to gain additional followers.

On the other side of the coin, posts that draw out negative reactions and comments—or that are shown to prompt followers to hide the post or unfollow your page altogether—can also be very instructive. The comments may tip leaders off to a program, policy, or personnel problem that should be reviewed.

It might also provide insight into misperceptions that exist in the community, guiding communication efforts to clear the air and provide accurate information on the topic. While negative reactions and comments should be taken seriously, they should also be understood in context of the overall percentage of reactions and responses to determine how large and serious an issue it might be.

It's natural to focus on negative comments or reactions and fail to see that they are a small minority of the overall engagements. This is no more useful to your strategy and success than focusing only on positive comments and ignoring the negative.

In the page management area of a Facebook page, the Insights Overview page provides a free virtual treasure trove of information in one table. At the bottom of the Overview page, the table of recent posts can be expanded to include as many posts as the administrator wants.

In the table, the columns include:

- Published—shows the day and time that a post was published
- Post—small thumbnail and link to the actual post
- Type—indicates what was posted, which is usually a photo, video, text, or link
- Targeting—who is the post shared with? In most cases, this will be public
- Reach—number of people who saw the post
- Engagement—any action on the post, clicks, reactions, shares, and comments
- Promote—link to pay for promotion of the post

When your posts are listed in the rows to allow for easy comparison, several strategic insights become immediately apparent. As you review this table, ask yourself these questions:

- What types of posts are receiving the most attention? Check reach and engagement to find them.
- What message or messages are reflected in the top posts? Do they focus on student achievements, on staff recognition, or something else?
- What type of content is posted? Are they mostly just text, or do they include photos and video?
- When were they posted? Are most of the posts with high reach numbers posted on weekdays, weekends, during the day, or during the evening?

The answers to these questions provide a clear direction for schools and districts to create the most engaging posts and send them out when they are most likely to be seen.

While similar in some ways, Twitter has an additional set of key metrics that can shift your use from tactical to strategic and valuable. There are three main areas to find useful analytical data—Account Home, Activity Dashboard, and Audience Insights Dashboard. The Account Home area provides a great overview of information, including:

- Impressions—measurement of the total number of views of a conversation
- Profile Visits—number of times users visited your profile page
- Mentions—every time a username is tagged on Twitter with the @ symbol
- Followers—number of users who are following the account

It also has a "Tweet Highlights" section that lists the Top Tweet (with the most engagement), Top Mention (Someone else's tweet that mentions your account), and Top Media Tweet (tweet that includes a photo or video).

While the highlights section reflects just the last twenty-eight days, it is a good idea to take note of any themes in the content types that receive the most engagement because this can guide your content decisions moving forward.

The Tweet Activity Dashboard contains a section that is very similar to Facebook's Overview Page, listing all the tweets in the past twenty-eight days in a table format that makes it easy to compare different tweets for impressions, engagements, and engagement rates (number of engagements divided by impressions).

These numbers are important because they tell a story about the intensity of interest in the content. A tweet might be seen by a lot of different people, but if they don't feel compelled to interact with it, the tweet will have a low engagement rate. A large reach with low engagement isn't necessarily a bad thing, but remember that your top social media goal should always be engagement.

Instagram and LinkedIn also contain analytical dashboards that can be scanned for insights. There are also a variety of paid of scheduling tools, such as Sprout Social, HootSuite, and Buffer, that allow administrators to manage multiple social media accounts and pre-schedule posts while also providing a wide variety of meaningful analytics.

While all of this data is very helpful to understand your audiences' engagement behaviors, it can be overwhelming to get started. The important first step is to understand what social media platform your audience is already using—and to share there.

Not only will those posts and tweets help you gain followers and build a social media community, but the data they generate will give you a baseline to review. Once the data begins to roll in, the social media analytics will start to provide actionable information.

There is no shortage of support for those hoping to collect and understand social media analytics. Whether you use free tutorial videos and articles or paid services, it is worth your time to learn about the social media work you are doing—what's working and what can be improved to maximize your investment of time and effort.

E-NEWSLETTERS

There are a number of online e-newsletter programs available for schools and districts, and they generally offer similar analytic information. The most important data questions you should ask with an e-newsletter begins with the how many of your families and stakeholders have an email address to receive your e-newsletter or internet or smartphone access to read it.

If these are barriers for even a small percentage of the population, it is important to choose an e-newsletter tool that also allows you to print out copies to provide to those audiences.

Once the e-newsletter is sent out, there is a wealth of data that will start to collect:

- How many people the e-newsletter was sent to
- How many people it didn't reach (bounce-backs due to blocked programs or incorrect email addresses)
- How many people opened the e-newsletter (open rate)
- How many people clicked on links provided in the e-newsletter (click rate)

Also, many e-newsletter programs also feature more sophisticated information, including which browsers and devices readers are using, when and who they forward the e-newsletter to, if they open it more than once, and when they open it.

Most commonly, open rates reflect the success of the subject line you use for your e-newsletter. Focus on words that will engage a busy parent, spark curiosity among your audience, and entice them to open the email.

Schools and districts may want to try a number of different approaches to increase the interest in opening the e-newsletter, from the basic "ABC Unified E-newsletter September 2018" to highlighting different items in the newsletter, such as "Catch up on Girls Soccer Highlights in This Month's E-newsletter" or "Jefferson Elementary Captured a Top STEM Award, Find out How!"

Understanding click rates tells you a lot about what your readers are most interested in learning more about. Consider including the first one to two paragraphs of a story in the newsletter and then link to the rest of it on the website or a social media page.

When someone is interested enough to find out more, that clicked link becomes part of your dataset and can be compared to the click rates of other items in the e-newsletter that month or any month.

KEY IDEAS IN THIS CHAPTER

- With nearly every digital-based program that schools and districts are utilizing to communicate, there is a wealth of information available—often for free.
- Creating a checklist of the key analytics in each system can simplify the process of regularly checking the numbers and make it a regular and expected part of the communication process.
- Remember, checking the data isn't just a good idea because it is a best practice; understanding what your audience wants and needs—and how it behaves—will tell you where to spend your precious time and energy.

CASE STUDY 7.1—HOW DO THEY REALLY FEEL?

During a recent eclipse, Park Hill School District Director of Communication Services Nicole Kirby was excited to be able to create an opportunity for students to integrate the experience with their classroom learning. The fact that Park Hill would be so close to the path of totality meant that it was truly going to be a unique experience.

Her team pulled together a comprehensive eclipse communication plan for parents and staff, understanding that there may be some concern about the event. The team developed messages that reassured families and described how the event would become a safe part of the learning experience that day.

One of the tactics in the plan included several social media posts leading up to the event and photos of the student activities that day.

Despite a robust communication effort, staff received a few phone calls that day from concerned citizens that felt the district should have canceled school that day to keep students safe. However, Kirby was able to point to an avalanche of data in the form of more than 700 positive reactions and 120 positive comments on the social media posts.

While there were a few concerned individuals, the community was for the most part very appreciative that Park Hill gave students the opportunity to learn from such a unique event.

CASE STUDY 7.2—GETTING IT JUST RIGHT

A combination of survey tools and analytics help Tuscaloosa City Schools perfect their voice messaging tool usage at the district and school level. One of Coordinator of Public Relations Lesley Bruinton's favorite questions on their annual survey is something she calls the "Goldilocks" question: Is the amount of information that families are receiving through the district's automated system too much, too little, or just right?

After years of collecting this same trend information, they found that maintaining an 80 percent "just right" is the best they can hope for and means they are doing a good job with the amount of messaging.

They also look at the analytics available in the messaging tool. When principals were leaving three or more messages a week, they found that no one was listening past forty seconds. They used that information to help their principals understand the "just right" amount of voice messaging.

Chapter Eight

Low(er) Tech Tracking Ideas

"I have been struck again and again by how important measurement is to improving the human condition."

—Bill Gates

While analytics is one of the easiest ways to collect data on communication efforts, there are other tools and systems that can help track efforts and make it easier to report on communication's less-visible activities.

For example, stakeholder groups and leadership can easily see the value in the work that goes into social media engagement and on-camera media interviews because they see the outputs or results.

However, they would likely have no reason to wonder about the time that goes into multiple phone calls and emails with a reporter to *keep* a negative story from making the news.

PR WORKSHEET

One of the easiest methods of creating an easy, systemic approach to communication planning is to implement a PR worksheet system. The first step in creating the worksheet is to identify every communication method for the school or district.

There is no method that is too informal to be included. For example, if there is a digital or even manual marquee sign in front of the property, list it. If the principal has a weekly coffee meeting or the superintendent likes to host brown-bag lunches, list them. Also list the regular go-to's, such as email, text, auto calls, social media platforms, the website, and so on.

Table 8.1.

Tool	Audience	Description	Due Date	Completed
Letter/flyer	Families	Sent home to families		
Flyer posted at sites	All	Break room, office		
Letter to staff	Internal	Through interoffice mail		
Events calendar	All	District website		
News item	All	District website		
School websites	All	News items		
Board email	Internal	Email to all members		
Leadership email	Internal	Email to administrators		
District email	Internal	Email to all staff		
Community email	All	Email to those sign up		
E-newsletter	All	Email with links		
Automated call	Families	District automated call system		
Automated text	Families	District system		
School site parent mtg	Families	Mtg for families		
School site staff mtg	Internal	Mtg for staff members		
School signage	All	Public signage in front		
Classroom mtg	Families	Mtg with families from one class		
Media advisory	All	Brief invite before event		
Media release	All	Details provided after the event		
Media story	All	Story written after the event		
District Facebook post	All	Post/photo/video		
School Facebook post	All	Post/photo/video		
Facebook ad	All	Paid ad or promoted post		
District Twitter post	All	Photo/video/share		
Brown-bag mtg	All	Bring lunch to mtg		
Parent mtg	Families	Mtg at district or school site		
Staff mtg	Internal	Mtg at district or school site		
DO signage	All	Public signage in front		

Once all of the communication tools are collected, identify the top one or two audiences that are reached through that channel. For example, brown-bag lunches would likely be staff while coffee clutches probably draw a lot of families.

Some, like television media, might be classified as "all." There is no right way to categorize the audiences. The audiences column should be revisited and tweaked as the system gets utilized.

Next, create a table in Microsoft Word, Google Docs, Excel, or Sheets worksheets. The first two columns will be "Audience" and "Tool," with other possible columns added to the right.

The other columns depend on how the worksheets are used but could include a description of the tool if there will be people in the school system that are not familiar with all of the communication methods.

Another column might be the due date for the activity to be completed and another might be a completed box to mark off what's been done. Schools or districts could also include a column for who is responsible for completing the activity as well as what the budget is for the item.

Table 8.1 provides an example of a district-level worksheet. It is very easy to create one for the school level as well.

As a Word document, the worksheet can be printed out and taken to meetings and filled out by hand. In Google Docs, it can be accessed online and shared with others in the meeting, filled out in a collaborative online effort, and remain accessible to everyone after the meeting.

In both of these cases, the worksheet serves as a brainstorming tool, facilitating a quick and easy mini-communication planning session with each big issue or decision. Many districts and schools using this approach have gotten into the habit of asking, "And how will this be communicated?" after each agenda item.

After the necessary communication activities have been identified and assigned, the sheets serve as a tracking tool to ensure that everything is getting done in a timely manner. After completion, it can serve as a reporting tool if the information from each sheet is collected.

In a spreadsheet format where each tab represents a worksheet and they are set up to total into a final tab, the reporting is even easier.

EMAIL FOLDERS

Another simple way to help keep track of the time associated with school communication is to save nearly every email. It is contrary to what most information technology departments would like to see, but holding on to emails provides an easy source of data and reporting material if organized effectively.

Creating a series of email folders is the first step. There are a couple of different ways to go about setting up the folder system, and it may take some adjustment after a period of time of using the system.

Creating and organizing folders based on core services or school sites is one way to categorize and track activities. For example, one of the most common district-level complaints is that one school feels that another is receiving more public relations attention than they are.

Creating school folders and saving emails to and from school sites can help measure and report on the equity of the assistance each school is receiving. It can also help with keeping track of the level of effort on the school's part. If the district-level staff is sending the same requests to all schools and yet there are a few that don't respond in a timely manner, the folders are one way to begin to notice that theme and prompt a conversation with school staff to improve the situation.

Another way to organize might be by issue. For example, media inquiries, boundary changes, events, and facilities improvements could all be overall folders with subfolders under each that contain email communication related to each one.

There is no right way to organize the folders. If there is some confusion about which way to go, collecting all communication-related emails in a general folder for a period of time and then combing through them for themes could suggest an organizational strategy.

One folder that will need to be included no matter the organizational structure is a crisis folder and subfolders under that folder for each crisis the school or district addresses that year. This is another area that is usually underestimated when it comes to the amount of time that school leaders and communicators are spending.

The volume of emails representing time spent can come as a big surprise to even the people that have been involved in working on lockdowns, addressing rumors, and dealing with illness outbreaks.

Once the folders are set up and the emails are being collected, the next step is to set up regular reporting categories. Like most of the tips in this chapter, there is no right answer when it comes to the categories selected.

They can and should vary based on the school or district. Is there a need to demonstrate the amount of work taking place on a particular project? Would it be helpful for board members to understand how much time is spent on special projects they've requested? How are other schools and districts reporting on their efforts?

With the data collected through the worksheet and folder systems, a number of different reports can be pulled together. For example, a monthly or annual report on support for each school, for each campaign or issue, or even by type of tool utilized. Table 8.2 provides some ideas about types of reporting data.

Low(er) Tech Tracking Ideas

Table 8.2.

Item	Data Source
# Media inquiries	Department media log
# Advisories sent	Email folders
# Stories sent	Email folders
# Stories posted on web	Web
# Website visits	Google Analytics
# Videos posted on web	Worksheets
# Automated calls	Call log from vendor
# Events covered	Worksheets
Community meetings attended	Reported from all departments
Public meetings hosted	Reported from all departments
Fact sheets produced	Worksheets
Surveys produced	Worksheets
Events held	Worksheets
Social media engagement	Social media platforms

The identification of report categories should be considered thoughtfully because what gets measured gets valued. When communication efforts are tracked, leaders and stakeholders begin to understand the importance of the function, the amount of work that goes into effective efforts, and the connection between engagement and learning. Chapter 9 provides more tips on reporting communication efforts.

KEY IDEAS IN THIS CHAPTER

- Tracking and reporting on communication efforts can help everyone in the organization appreciate the value of the activities.
- There are easy, low-tech ways to collect information about a school or district's communication efforts.
- Worksheets and folders can help school leaders categorize, track, and report on communication at all levels.

CASE STUDY 8.1—DATA DRIVES PRESCHOOL EFFORT

The Eudora School District had a vision of universal preschool that would provide a solid foundation for all students coming into kindergarten. The vision wasn't that the district would provide all the preschool services, but rather that the small community would create a tapestry of public–private partnerships with slots for all children in Eudora, Kansas.

In the process of seeking out funding for the vision, district leaders decided to apply for a grant and called together a summit of key local preschool providers. During the summit, they proposed the vision and listened.

Providers shared excitement about the opportunity to work together and also voiced frank concerns about the district creating unfair competition. One provider in particular even shed tears because she was so anxious about the impact on the preschool she ran. The group talked through the range of concerns and discussed how they could share professional development for staff and transportation for students.

Eudora Director of Communications Kristin Magette credits the format—an open group feedback process—for their ability to work through even the sticky issues.

At the next feedback opportunity, which was purposefully shared with preschool providers and their families and open to anyone in the community, they collected additional input.

There was a moderator at each of the five tables and participants cycled through the different tables. Each table hosted a unique topic, such as barriers to partnerships or transportation ideas.

"It was much better than typical town hall forum," explains Magette. "A lot of people who have great ideas don't speak, and this format kept a small group of people from dominating the discussion."

The information district leaders collected during the summit also helped inform a survey of stakeholders to ensure that the feedback on the issues was representative of the larger community.

Chapter Nine

Making Data Accessible

"Maybe stories are just data with a soul."

—Brené Brown

Most people have no background or experience in understanding numbers as large as a school or district budget. They come to board meetings to try to serve as good citizens and get bombarded with millions and hundreds of millions in budget figures and large tables of numbers that make any average person want to run for the hills.

It is part of the job to explain large numbers, and when schools and districts do it well, it guides communities to make good decisions for students.

One of the most basic tenets of communication is to consider the audience. What is the demographic, educational, and cultural experience of the people you are talking to? If they don't have everyday experience working with budgets in the millions, what do they have experience with that can serve as an accurate analogy?

Analogies serve as a bridge for communicators, a bridge between the concept they need to describe and the experiences and perceptions of the audience. For example, while most families would have a hard time understanding making cuts in the $10 million range, they might be able to understand an analogy as a percentage of a household budget.

In addition to the percentage, make it even more explicit by saying, for example in the case of a 10 percent cut, that it is similar to a family with a monthly household income of $4,000 having to make monthly cuts of $400, which is not an easy thing to do.

Another helpful household analogy is around one-time spending versus ongoing spending that dips into savings. Setting up a scenario where a household has a savings account with $3,000 in it and is considering a new expense (say the lease of a new vehicle) that costs $300 a month. The family won't be able to pay for that car very long and needs to stick to purchasing something that falls in line with their monthly budget to be sustainable.

Moving to a school-based analogy, another idea is to compare large amounts to the number of teachers (or any position) that could be hired with that same amount.

For example, a group may be pushing for a new program that costs $900,000. If the annual cost of an average teacher in the district is $70,000, it is helpful to say it is equivalent to nearly thirteen teachers. Be sure to include the benefits costs in that analogy to make it accurate.

Other school-based comparisons might be one classroom's annual budget, one school's annual budget, and the cost to educate one student in a year or one student over their educational career.

Another helpful tool in talking about budgets that makes them easier to understand is to look at the percentages in spending against one dollar. Even though the amounts are significantly different, everyone can relate to a dollar, and when eighty cents of that dollar goes toward staffing costs, that doesn't leave a lot of money for other things.

This is a natural concept for a graphic: cutting a dollar into appropriate-to-the-percentage-size pieces and labeling the cost centers, such as teachers, support staff, administrators, curriculum, facilities, and so on.

INFOGRAPHICS

Speaking of graphics, one of the ways to communicate numbers in a way that is more fun and engaging than a table or list is to create an infographic. While it may sound like it must take a lot of design or technical expertise, there are many programs, such as Piktochart, Canva, and Lucidpress, that can provide creative and inexpensive templates to meet every need. They also offer educator pricing.

Figure 9.1 is an example of an infographic that describes the results of a district's communication survey results. This infographic was created using a template in Piktochart, updating the numbers to reflect the district's story.

Remembering to tell a story is extremely important in developing an infographic. It isn't about simply reporting all the data that would be included in an overall report but rather selecting the pieces of data that show something insightful, interesting, or unexpected.

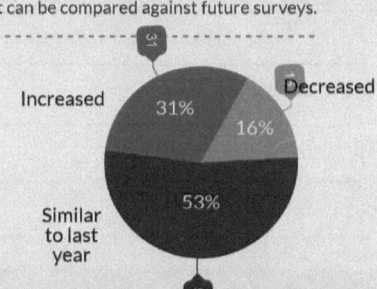

Figure 9.1. Sample infographic reflecting Amador County Public School's annual survey results

In a survey report, all the question responses need to be reviewed, but when creating graphics around the data, it's OK to be selective as long as people know where to find the longer report. Graphics tell a story *based* on the data that is selected.

If people need to be convinced that there is a growing academic gap based on economic need and the district data supports that narrative, it should be highlighted. The placement, color, and size of the items tell the audience how important that item is.

Make sure your data graphics are intentional, highlighting the statistics you want them to.

Graphics can be so much more impactful than numbers alone. Figure 9.2 shows a table with the results of a question about perceptions of how well the district communicates with families and the same information in an infographic block with two large arrows.

While the table is clear in presenting the numbers associated with two years of responses on the question, the infographic representation of the same numbers is simpler and bolder. Readers can understand the contrast between the two years very quickly when they are looking at the graphic.

Question	2016	2017	Change	
Doesn't tell us much about what's going on	19%	7%	↓3	
Gives us a limited amount of information	48%	24%	↓24	-33
Keeps us adequately informed	24%	30%	↓6	
Keeps us fairly well informed	6%	26%	↑20	+29
Keeps us fully informed	3%	12%	↑9	

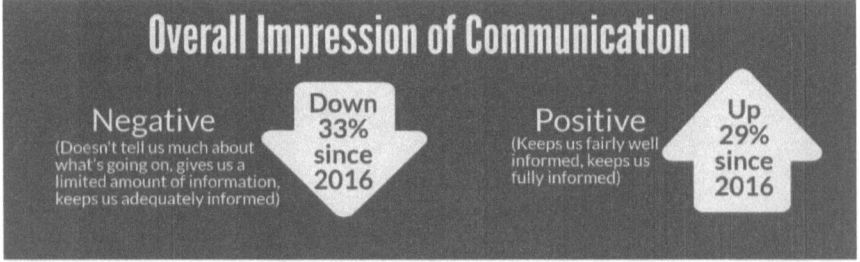

Figure 9.2. Comparison of data displayed in a table format versus an infographic

REPORTING

After thoughtfully pulling the data together in a format that tells a story and is accessible for families and other stakeholders, the next step is to ensure that it is distributed as widely as possible. Unfortunately, this is the step that is most often overlooked even when districts take the time to do the research and measure their efforts. A lot of effort goes into the collecting, and once it is posted on the school or district website, the box is checked.

Doing the valuable work of collecting data in district surveys or through the methods described in Chapters 7 and 8 (analytics and low-tech tracking ideas) is something that school leaders should brag about—not just to demonstrate their responsiveness to stakeholders, but also to reinforce that they value listening and evidence-based ideas and actions.

When audiences see that their participation has had an effect, they are more likely to participate in future engagement activities and more likely to feel connected to their school and district.

Just like data collection, data report distribution doesn't have to involve a lot of additional work. The monthly and annual reports discussed in Chapter 8 could be shared in a variety of communication channels, likely the same ones identified in the worksheet approach in that same chapter.

Also, they can be posted on a website with a link to them in an email signature line, perhaps with a lead-in such as "Thanks for participating in our recent community survey; see the results here" or "Want to see how hard we're working to keep you updated? Check out our October report here."

If there is a specific department in the district responsible for communication, create a one-pager of the annual data and have it displayed or readily available in-person or on the department website. If the communication functions are part of the principal or superintendent offices, provide access there.

Make sure internal audiences know about the work happening. Schedule communication training with other departments to expand the number of people with the skills needed to engage families and other stakeholders.

Social media is also a great place to highlight the work that is happening. Links to survey results and tracking statistics can be utilized for a series of posts by focusing on surprising findings or findings that resulted in changes. It can also start insightful conversations with the community.

One last idea is specifically for districts that have board meetings that utilize closed session time. Often, community attendees are waiting for the end of the closed session period, and this is a perfect time to provide rotating slides of important findings and statistics.

There are likely a number of places in which people are waiting or gathering for another reason that can also serve as a forum for sharing the data. All it takes is a little creativity to identify the opportunities.

KEY IDEAS IN THIS CHAPTER

- When talking about large numbers that are difficult for families and other stakeholders to understand, use helpful analogies.
- Use graphics and infographics to highlight the most important statistics; they are easy to create through the use of templates.
- Don't forget to share the results of research methods and statistics on the communication work happening at the school and district level.

CASE STUDY 9.1—MAKING NUMBERS ACCESSIBLE

When you're talking about large budgets, people can get overwhelmed. To make the numbers more accessible, Kelly Avants, chief communication officer at Clovis Unified, looks at them through the eyes of the audience and tries to find a common denominator, such as "What would the impact be to one school?" or comparisons to a home budget. "We have to make big numbers real to people, or they simply tune out."

She also believes infographics are helpful, especially for the English-language learner audience. Clovis Unified used infographics for their series of Local Control Accountability Plan (LCAP) meetings, and post-meeting surveys gave the visual pieces high marks.

The graphics helped explain how money was being spent, services to students, and the variety of funding sources in the district.

Chapter Ten

Qualitative Research, Understanding the Richness of Experience

> "I want to understand the world from your point of view. I want to know what you know in the way you know it. I want to understand the meaning of your experience, to walk in your shoes, to feel things as you feel them, to explain things as you explain them. Will you become my teacher and help me understand?"
>
> —James P. Spradley

Qualitative research sometimes doesn't get the respect it deserves. It is messy, it doesn't provide black-and-white solutions, and it doesn't easily translate into a statistical report that makes people feel good.

However, it can provide insights that would never be uncovered by a simple multiple-choice survey. If you are interested in the scope of the problem, use quantitative research; if the interest is on the nature of the problem, use qualitative research.

While many of these qualitative research methods might not be able to provide high-confidence generalizations about populations, they all can provide unique value under the right circumstances.

Qualitative methods provide a richness of understanding that is impossible to get from quantitative methods alone. Qualitative methods give us the words and phrases that our audiences are using and sometimes bring up questions we might not think to ask.

With qualitative methods, the researcher has to let go of a certain amount of control and follow where the experience leads. While in most cases there are replicable data collection procedures (such as checklists, questionnaires, and facilitator guides) that ask for similar input from participants, the researcher has to be comfortable with exploring the topic rather than confirming their thinking about the topic. It can be uncomfortable for some people, but it is an excellent source of real-life, participant-driven feedback.

The key to obtaining the best input qualitative research is choosing the right research tool. Just like developing an effective four-step PR plan, school leaders need to be sensitive to the problem, the multiple audiences, the best applicable research method, and how the questions and tools may need to be tailored differently for each audience.

Let's review some of the qualitative methods available for examining different issues in school communication. Table 10.1 includes a description of a variety of methods and examples of each.

Table 10.1.

Method	Description	Examples
Direct Observation	Watching activity or touring an area and taking notes about what is happening	Observing student behavior in front of campus, observing pick up and drop off, secret shopper
Interview	Sitting down with a subject matter expert, impacted audience, or influencer	Talking with a parent who transferred out of district, talking with a school leader who has experienced a similar issue
Case Study	Intense study of a specific person or example	Developing a description of how a crisis was handled in a neighboring district, developing a description of how one student changed their academic circumstances through hard work
Focus Group	Bringing representatives of a group together to discuss a particular topic or preview messages	Group of students come together to discuss new dress code policy, group of teachers come together to discuss restorative justice
Open-Ended Question	Questions requiring a text answer on a survey	Anything else you would like to tell us?
Advisory Group	Ongoing informal gathering of people willing to provide helpful critical feedback	Curriculum and instruction group, communication and PR group

DIRECT OBSERVATION

There are a number of valuable qualitative methods that can be easily undertaken. One is simply direct observation. Receive a complaint about the way that students are behaving in front of the campus after school each day? Park across the street for a few days as school gets out and observe the activity for patterns.

To formalize it, create a checklist to use while observing and mark on the list what happens—while the observational approach is qualitative in nature, adding up the observed behavior on the checklist turns it into quantitative data.

Is there a specific area that could use an after-school staff assignment? Were the students well-behaved? Maybe the concerned caller caught the school on a bad day. Either way, observing what is happening will provide the answers.

INTERVIEW

Another qualitative option that can be very helpful is an interview with someone impacted by the issue or perhaps a subject-matter expert in the area. It's a good idea to start with an initial set of questions on the topic, but be sure to leave room for unstructured discussion.

With questions such as, "Is there anything else about this I should know?" or "Is there anything else you want to share?" the answers can bring out a lot of valuable information. The use of open-ended questions leads to much richer conversation and deeper understanding than closed-ended questions.

The interviewee is free to move the conversation in any direction, and the discoveries can be surprising. While the school or district leader may think a particular issue is about one thing, such as budget cuts, perhaps some stakeholder groups may think it is about something else entirely, such as respect for teacher input.

Interviewing other school leaders that have been through an experience or conducted a campaign similar to the one you are considering is another great example of qualitative research. There is no reason to recreate the wheel when undertaking a new campaign. In most cases, there are many other schools and districts that have implemented communication campaigns that can provide valuable lessons learned or even specific strategies and tactics.

CASE STUDIES

Case studies, one of the key research methods for this book, are another example of qualitative research. A case study is an intensive study of a specific individual or context. It examines specific samples to better understand a phenomenon that occurs more broadly. Case studies are often used as a follow up when school or district leaders find themes reflected in quantitative data that they want to better understand.

For example, one district discovered that one of the biggest dips in enrollment was occurring between sixth and seventh grade, when students moved from the elementary campus to the junior high school. A district administrator reached out to one of the families that left the district the year before and developed a case study on their experience that shed light on a number of issues at the elementary and junior high schools. The case study was shared with principals at all district schools as an example of the importance of customer service and building positive perceptions of district schools. One of the downsides of a case study is that some of the people who may need to learn the lessons from it will think it is limited in scope and doesn't apply to them. However, when presented in conjunction with representative quantitative data, it can be very powerful.

FOCUS GROUPS

Another qualitative method that is well understood by most people is focus groups. Fundamentally, they are group interviews usually conducted with people who have a common experience, such as those participants that are all preschool teachers.

Interviews can be as informal as inviting some students into a room with some snacks to talk about an issue or as formal as hosting a group at a testing facility with one-way glass that allows researchers to watch the group underway.

They can be used as formative research as strategies and messages are being developed, as a pretest when strategies and messaging are ready to be launched, and as an evaluative method after a campaign to determine the impact it had and even the perception of the campaign itself.

Some simple guidelines will ensure that focus groups are as effective as possible. The list of questions for the group should be developed and reviewed ahead of time to ensure they will get at the information that is needed.

Pretesting the list of questions with someone who is similar to the focus group participants can be very helpful. As with developing a good survey, it's important to avoid unnecessary jargon and not be too prescriptive. The more open the questions are, the more unexpected and potentially meaningful the feedback might be.

During the group session, the facilitator should ensure that no one member is dominating the conversation or making it uncomfortable for others to participate in the discussion. Creating a comfortable atmosphere is essential to getting good input. To that end, the first few questions on the list should be easy warm-ups, avoiding topics that might be polarizing until later in the session.

It is also a good idea to have multiple focus groups to be able to compare reactions and elicit the range of possible responses (feelings, perceptions, knowledge, attitudes, etc.) to the questions or messages. Getting people to participate in groups can be challenging; consider offering childcare, refreshments, and stipends to make it more attractive to prospective participants.

OPEN-ENDED QUESTIONS

When school leaders opt to include open-ended questions on a survey that is mostly quantitative, it adds more work to the survey analysis but also provides the opportunity to learn something outside of what was expected. Some examples of open-ended questions include:

- Are there any other thoughts you want to share about our district?
- Is there any other communication tool we should be using to reach you?
- What is the best thing about your child's school?
- Do you have any suggestions for our communication team?
- What else do you need to know about this issue that has not been mentioned here?

Asking open-ended questions is not for the faint of heart. There might be some difficult or even mean-spirited feedback, and there will also be some nonsensical or nonresponsive content. However, there will likely also be some gems that reveal information that would never have been discovered in a multiple-choice question.

Analysis of open-ended questions can be time-consuming. It involves collecting all the feedback and organizing it by theme and also taking note of how often the same comment was made to ascertain how representative the content might be.

Sometimes qualitative research isn't even a conscious, formalized research effort but rather just a smart way to become informed. For example, it is usually a good idea to seek out diverse viewpoints, particularly on a polarizing issue. Many school leaders make a habit of developing a group of "critical friends" that they meet with regularly to preview ideas and help anticipate potential challenges.

Qualitative methods complement quantitative research. When conducted first, qualitative methods help us determine the questions to ask quantitatively to find out if what we learned in the small-scale applies to the population at large. After a quantitative effort, qualitative research can also draw out details that are impossible to explore in other ways. In fact, the two types of research together may be the best recipe for effective decision-making.

KEY IDEAS IN THIS CHAPTER

- Qualitative methods give us the words and phrases that our audiences are using and sometimes bring up questions we didn't think to ask.
- There are a number of qualitative methods that can be used to determine the nature of the problem and connect directly with the affected audiences.
- Qualitative and quantitative research methods complement each other, answering different questions.

CASE STUDY 10.1—BARTERING FOCUS GROUP FACILITATION CONTAINS COSTS, GETS THE JOB DONE

Just prior to Y2K and upon hiring a new superintendent, Pearl River Schools (NY) embarked on a comprehensive needs assessment to inform planning for the year 2000 and beyond.

With the goal to determine priorities of students, staff, parents, and community members, Community Relations Director Sandy Cokeley, APR, proposed both quantitative surveys and focus groups. While fellow administrators embraced the idea, no budget provision existed to support their deployment.

Having been in her role with the district for ten years and knowing that an impartial, trained facilitator was key to the success of focus groups, Cokeley acknowledged she could not facilitate the groups herself.

During a conversation with a former colleague from a prior agency who had since moved to corporate public relations, they arrived at a mutually beneficial concept—facilitate focus groups in each other's agencies. Both were trained, experienced public relations practitioners. Both of their agencies were seeking research. And both of their administrations agreed to the barter, freeing up time for each to work in the other's agency.

The end result for Pearl River Schools was reliable, qualitative data on preferences and priorities from representatives of student, parent, staff, and community audiences. Cokeley then used the input to frame the quantitative follow-up surveys that she developed and conducted internally.

Together, the research provided Pearl River leaders with the solid information they needed to map out a relevant and responsive strategic plan for the turn of the century while reinforcing the value of their investment in the Community Relations Office.

CASE STUDY 10.2—CRITICAL FRIENDS

Qualitative input is one of the most important tools at the communication department's disposal at Peel District School Board. Director of Communications Carla Pereira and the entire team makes an effort to identify and seek input from what they call "critical friends."

These are stakeholders that may have short- or long-term concerns or issues with the district. The Peel District reaches out to hear that kind of critical feedback first before developing a communication plan.

"We value constructive input—it's much more valuable than hearing from folks who always tell us everything is fine," explains Pereira.

In addition to specific issue groups, the team meets with regular advisory groups that contain members who will offer frank, genuine input. Pereira works to draw out their perspectives and stories that tell her just as much about a topic as the quantitative data.

Chapter Eleven

When the Data Is Hard to Swallow

"You can't always get what you want, but if you try sometimes, yeah you might find you get what you need!"

—Keith Richards and Mick Jagger

Sometimes when we go through the process of collecting data about an issue, it doesn't come back the way we predict it will. This can put the data collector in a tricky position, especially if the school or district leadership team is already heading down a path based on the data coming back differently.

For example, the district is planning to make a change in the starting schedule for all schools and sends out a survey asking families about the change. When the survey results come back in, a huge concern emerges.

Most of the families leave for full-time jobs well before the new, later time and would find it difficult to find childcare for the hour difference. The leadership team has already started planning for the change, and there are a number of good reasons to make the change, so what should happen next?

WHEN IN DOUBT, MORE RESEARCH

The first step is to keep an open mind. If there is any question that the results might not be fully representative or may be biased in some way, conduct some additional research.

For example, in the case of the schedule survey, it may help to tease out the details of families' objections to the schedule change and brainstorm ideas to solve the challenges of the change. Bringing together a series of groups of parents from different schools and at various grade levels to talk more in-depth about the issue could provide a lot of insight on the challenges as well as potential solutions.

If the elementary schools were to offer before-school childcare and tutoring, the concerns about the schedule change could be minimized. Even after a potential solution is discovered, it's likely a good idea to circle back around with a quantitative method to confirm that the proposed solution will work for the majority of families.

IT'S JUST INFORMATION

However, many times the solution to the situation won't be so tidy. Sometimes the data that comes back is indicative of a change that the school or district needs to make. It's important not to be defensive and to keep an open mind about what the data is suggesting.

Even if it is presented in a way that is very harsh or difficult, from a systemic perspective, it is just information. It may be information the school or district desperately needs to know. As Winston Churchill once said, "Criticism may not be agreeable, but it is necessary. It fulfills the same function as pain in the human body. It calls attention to an unhealthy state of things. If it is heeded in time, danger may be averted; if it is suppressed, a fatal distemper may develop."

Negative data can tell us a number of things—it might suggest that we need to change a program or policy, provide personnel training, or increase communication to clear up a misunderstanding. It takes a healthy organization and leadership to be vulnerable enough to look at the information and recognize the need for change rather than disregard or undercut the results.

As the data collector and researcher, you have asked for opinions and input, sometimes from audiences who might lack the skills or confidence to provide their feedback in other, more explicit ways.

It is part of the responsibility of a school leader to listen to these voices and champion them, even when it's difficult. Perhaps *especially* when it is difficult. Being courageous and listening to stakeholders means following the data even when it crosses leadership beliefs.

INTERNAL REFLECTION

To take it a step further, organizational leaders should think about applying data to internal areas as well; for example, an analysis of how money is allocated that includes where staff spends their time.

It is said that our budget reflects our values, but many times there are issues and areas receiving much more attention and energy than people realize. An audit of how time is utilized in a department can be extremely enlightening. Table 11.1 is a partial example of a district's audit of their communication department.

Table 11.1.

Communications Department Staff Cost by Function

Crisis Communication Support	Director time 15%	$20,000.00
Revise district crisis communication plan	Specialist time 5%	$4,757.65
Respond to and manage media	Assistant time 2%	$1,114.40
On-site support as needed		
Letters for families and staff		
Call scripts for families and staff		
Discussion points for families and staff	Total	$25,872.05
School Site Marketing and Promotion	Director time 5%	$6,667.40
School fact sheets and brochures	Specialist time 20%	$19,030.06
Event planning advice/assistance	Videographer time 60%	$46,149.06
Event photography and videography	Assistant time 12%	$6,686.40
Inspiring school banners	Total	$78,532.92
District-Wide Issue Communication	Director time 20%	$26,669.60
Fact sheets and flyers	Specialist time 15%	$14,272.95
Discussion points	Videographer time 5%	$3,845.80
Powerpoint creation and design	Assistant time 5%	$2,786.00
Letter creation and review		
Event marketing and planning		
Automated Calls	Total	$47,574.35
Web Content and Development	Director time 5%	$6,667.40
(Home page, Communications section, News	Specialist time 20%	$19,030.60
items section, Events section, Spotlight	Videographer time 5%	$3,845.80
section, Special web sections by issue,	Assistant time 5%	$2,786.00
school site news sections)		
Training for department webmasters		
Auditing of content		
Video stories	Total	$32,330.60
Media and Community Relations	Director time 25%	$33,337.00
Advisories and Releases	Specialist time 5%	$4,757.65
Response to inquiries—average 3 per week	Videographer time 5%	$3,845.80
Press conference coordination	Assistant time 12%	$6,686.40
3rd party flyer approval		
Community event booth coordination		
Business partner development		
Community group liaison	Total	$48,626.85
Recognition/Morale Activities	Director time 10%	$13,334.80
Classified School Employees of the Year	Specialist time 20%	$19,030.60
Program	Videographer time 10%	$7,691.60
Teachers of the Year Program Coordination	Assistant time 40%	$21,730.80
Annual Spring Neighborhood School		
Celebrations		
Annual Employee Welcome and Wellness Fest	Total	$61,787.80

When the budget is broken up in this way, it can shed a lot of light on the unintended priorities of a school or district. With intentional focus, the attention can shift to other areas or the organization can come to accept the areas that are requiring so much staff time.

For example, the department appears to spend the most time and staff resources in the area of school site promotion—something that is very helpful for stakeholders to be aware of, particularly if they are critical of the expenditures in the communication department.

If the promotional efforts result in the recruitment of additional families, the return on investment can wipe out any financial investment in communication.

Another idea to use data to increase transparency is a customer service survey of families and school site employees to rate the service levels of district office departments. This is an extremely vulnerable and courageous step to take and hopefully reflects a sincere interest in improving service to families and schools.

One of the surprising outcomes in some of these surveys is the difference in how departments are perceived by families versus school staff. When the results come back, any customer service training can incorporate specific weak areas and provide examples that hit the mark.

KEY IDEAS IN THIS CHAPTER

- If the data comes back and it is unexpected or in doubt, conduct more research to confirm the original results.
- Don't be afraid of negative data; it is information that can help improve organizational systems.
- Use data to be as transparent as possible with finances and service with internal time audits and surveys.
- Data can't solve all problems, but it can free up the time to apply personal talents to other challenges.

CASE STUDY 11.1—MOVE AWAY FROM WEBSITES

Peel District School Board used to spend a lot of time and resources on their school websites. Thanks to the amount of data they collect and analyze, the communications team has shifted away from this common tactic.

After looking at declining or stagnant page views and little engagement, they now spend more of their time and energy on voice and text messaging, only referring stakeholders to school websites when there is a lot of content that needs to be communicated.

Even in those cases, they use a voice or text message to direct families to the specific content area on the site.

CASE STUDY 11.2—MOVING FROM VOICE TO TEXT

Sometimes the data from one source contradicts the data from another source. When it comes to preferred communication methods in the Eudora School District, that is exactly what happened.

As part of surveys, families are most likely to say that they prefer email, but through the analytics, district leaders know that families are most likely to open a text message.

Kristin Magette, director of communication, uses both. When it is important, she sends a text message that indicates there is important information about an issue and asks the receiver to check their email for details.

Chapter Twelve

No PR Person, No Problem!

"Teamwork divides that tasks and multiplies the success."

—Author Unknown

If you're not lucky enough to have a dedicated public relations professional at your school or district, this chapter is for you. It will also likely be helpful for small, one-person shops. While having an internal PR pro is ideal, there are some benefits to engaging a wider variety of departments and people in the effort.

One of the downsides of having a communication or public relations department is that it sometimes is an excuse for everyone else to ignore the area. Even in districts that have the luxury of a large PR department, it should be emphasized that PR is a function that everyone is responsible for, not one person or department.

When there is no department to turn to, everyone will need to take on the responsibility, and that's an opportunity. When there are more departments and people involved, there is more diversity in the voices that are included and more perspectives based on different roles in the organization.

INTEGRATED APPROACH

Sometimes that can result in a more integrated approach to an issue and help identify issues that a PR department might not see. For example, in the case of developing a campaign around improving perception, a transportation director might rightfully point out that a bus driver is the first face many students see. Providing customer service training and support might not have been the top priority of others in the room, but it is a great idea.

Another example might be a recruitment campaign. While it is natural for the human resources team to be associated with recruitment, principals and staff in curriculum and instruction are likely able to chime in with a lot of information about what they have heard from new teachers and staff.

For example, what are the strengths of the school or district that made the difference when it came to choosing the job? Those are the message points of any recruitment campaign.

SPECIALIZATION

There may also be some natural specialization of tasks associated with communication. For example, the administrative assistant to the superintendent may already be tracking any media mention of the district.

Instead of just sending it to the leadership team, the assistant could be trained to analyze the media piece using the rubric in the templates section of this book and keep a spreadsheet of the mentions with a classification of whether the story was positive, neutral, or negative.

Analytics are incredibly helpful when it comes to decision-making and planning out communication efforts. A district or school technology person is probably the best bet for finding someone that can access the data in the technology systems. They may also be able to better interpret and report out the analytics than the average staff person.

SYSTEMIC APPROACH

The worksheet approach that was shared in Chapter 8 is a great tool to use when there are many people sharing the PR duties. Used as a paper copy or electronically on a laptop or even a smartphone makes it very easy to brainstorm ideas, track efforts, and spread the work among several people.

At the school and district level, it's helpful if the leadership teams can get into a habit of communicating out events, programs, and decisions that are discussed at meetings. Certain people can become experts at specific tools, and once the key message is developed, it is simply modified to use in multiple formats.

One of the critical items to facilitating a systemic approach to communication is to provide training to a wide variety of staff members. In a smaller district in rural California, the classified managers recently received an hour-long smartphone video and social media training.

When the facilities manager is out reviewing the latest installation of solar panels, he doesn't need to ask someone else to join him to take the video and then post to the district's Facebook account. He pulls out his smartphone and it can be posted in minutes.

Teachers have opportunities each day to capture the magical moments that are happening in the classroom. The latest STEM experiment can be online before students return home, providing parents with the answer to their age-old question, "What did you learn today?"

Don't have the expertise in your school or district? There are a number of school communication consultants that can be tapped to come in and provide a variety of training, from social media to customer service and crisis communication preparation.

No money for a consultant? Pay attention to the organizations and businesses in your community that are proficient with social media. Perhaps there is a larger district nearby with a communication department. Many times reaching out to them with a request for a free training session will be met very positively.

Most importantly, don't worry about creating "perfect" videos or other social media content. The tone and intention are more important than how polished it looks. A simple video from a teacher of an inspiring art class doesn't have to be technically impressive to inspire.

What's important is to tell your story. While it should be enough that your school or district is doing a fantastic job educating students, the reality is that the expectations have changed.

There are more educational options than ever before. Young people don't necessarily attend the school in their neighborhood. Sharing the good things that are happening will keep your school or district competitive while connecting families and stakeholders to the learning process.

SOCIAL MEDIA

Social media is changing the way school communities work, offering a new model to engage with families, staff, students, and the world at large—if we take advantage of it. At schools throughout the United States, interaction through social media is building stronger, more successful relationships and creating the opportunities to have important conversations about the work we are doing.

As discussed in Chapters 2 and 3, one of the most important steps in the four-step public relations process is research. Research helps communicators to understand where the audience is and how to reach them.

If a significant portion of your school or district audience is on a specific social media platform, it is important to be there as well. As a critical part of family and community life, your school or district is being discussed on social media. If you're not on the same platforms, your voice won't be a part of the conversation.

It's understandable that some school leaders would prefer to avoid social media. They may not be confident in using it, fear online criticism, or don't think they have the time to take on one more thing.

Perhaps they believe that if they don't have a social media presence that they can avoid the potentially negative online exchanges. Unfortunately, what happens is that the school or district is still discussed online on social media platforms, but without a presence, they lose the ability to provide information, correct misperceptions, or even just "listen" to the concerns.

Immediate Response

One of the most significant implications of social media for government agencies is the public's expectation of accessibility and an immediate response. Whether it is a security concern, addressing a rumor, or providing event photos, families are expecting to receive information or a response in a much faster time frame than before social media was used.

In fact, there are many cases in which an issue has gone "viral" and expanded into the national news before an agency has been able to respond. Maintaining a social media presence increases the likelihood that your staff will know about an issue before the national news.

Reinforce Messaging

Rather than creating new content specifically for each social media platform, schools and districts should think of Twitter or Facebook as just one more tool. If there is a story or captioned photo you would already be posting to a website or next month's newsletter, push that same content out to your social media platforms where appropriate.

While it is tempting to think audiences might tire of seeing the same information in multiple places, the reality is that it can take several impressions before they actually pay attention to it. Social media can help reinforce the information you are trying to get out in other ways.

Social Media Platforms

This is a difficult section to place in a book because social media as an industry is subject to a lot of fluctuation and is entirely dependent on changing audience preferences. It's another reason that conducting annual research into audience preferences is so important. So, at the risk of dating this material, here are a few of the current top platforms for schools.

Facebook—Use it as a place to post pictures, give updates, promote new initiatives, and answer questions. It's one of the best outlets for providing your supportive stakeholders with regular information they will be interested in.

Twitter—With less flexibility, be brief. Also, be quick. If it happened yesterday, it's old news on Twitter. Follow other organizations that might have appropriate content. It allows you to maintain a presence by sharing their content.

Instagram—Best for visual content and easiest to share across other channels. Whether it's a quick picture at a school event or a photo you've scheduled to post in advance, a quick adjustment on your Instagram settings menu will automatically distribute that same content to your choice of popular social media platforms, including those mentioned here.

LinkedIn—Create and maintain a professional profile to connect with current and potential employees and partners. You can network, share professional advice, and even recruit new talent.

If your school or district is just getting started on social media, you may want to start with just one or two platforms—those that your survey respondents rated highest. Once you gain some confidence with those, take the same content you are using and adjust to expand the reach of your messaging.

Why is this important? Messaging, when done well, takes time. If you are going to take the time to create the messaging for one or two places, it is not a lot more effort to modify the content for other places and get a much bigger bang for your buck. Table 12.1 provides an example of just that.

Content Ideas

If you're convinced and ready to get onto social media, you may be overwhelmed by the next step: generating content ideas. Here are few to get you started.

Weekly social media features—Consider adding weekly social media features (such as Wellness Wednesday) that your online community can look forward to. Taking part in popular social media trends can allow you to consistently post each day of the week and get your followers engaged and ready for the week ahead.

Table 12.1.

September	Facebook	Twitter	Instagram	LinkedIn
Good study habits/tips	Study tips for the year: Organize your study space, take regular breaks, and get a study partner. What are your tips? (photo/video of studying)	Check out these helpful tips to study this year. http://tinyurl.com/zgc48rg	A picture of students studying in the library with a caption of their favorite study tip	Top study tips from ABC Unified teachers
Donate to the education foundation	Video of principals, teachers, and students all discussing how they've benefited; link to donate	Donating to schools is a great way to give back (link of where to donate)	Photo/video of activities funded by the foundation and link to donate	Why donating to education is important
Grandparents Day	Share photos and reasons why your grandparents are the best with us! #ABCUnifiedGrandparents	What have you learned from your grandparents? Let us know using #ABCUnifiedGrandparents	Pictures from grandparents night event #ABCUnifiedGrandparents	Article about grandparents with tie-in to ABC Unified event
National Read a Book Day	Today is National Read a Book Day! Here are some of our favorite books . . . picture of some of the schools libraries	Its National Read a Book Day! What book are you reading today? #ABCUnifiedReads	Picture of students reading a book with National Read a Book Day caption #ABCUnifiedReads	List of ABC Unified top books for each age
Arts experience	Photo/video and description of an art experience in ABC Unified #ABCUnifiedInspires	Here is some of the art our students produced this month (pictures of students with art) #ABCUnifiedInspires	Pictures of students and their art #ABCUnifiedInspires	How art relates to science and math careers, arts in the district

You probably don't want to use one every day; three to four a week is enough, and never more than one "weekday" hashtag per day. Please see Table 12.2 for ideas.

Take over days—One great way to freshen and revitalize your content is to invite stakeholders to "take over" your feed and post from their perspective. That could include a principal, a teacher, a student, a board member, a community member, or a local business owner.

Inspiration from other agencies—Sharing quality content from other districts or organizations is a double win. It provides something useful for your audiences and strengthens the relationship with the outside entity which could lead to your posts being shared.

"Day of the Year" and other calendar tie-ins—There are a number of celebrations throughout the year that can inspire post ideas. The California Department of Education has a list at www.cde.ca.gov/re/pn/fb/cdecalendar.asp.

Tie into national conversations—For example, research released on graduation rates, college acceptance, and other student statistics. Post how your district is doing along with tips for how families can improve outcomes for their child.

Table 12.2.

Day	Hashtag/Post
Monday	#MondayFunday—staff having fun at work
	#MondayMotivation—inspirational quotes to start the week off
	#MusicMonday—school music programs and events
Tuesday	#TransformationTuesday—a split before/after photo, great for showing progress over time
	#TipTuesday—share your knowledge and advice
	#TuesdayTreat—highlight a "treat" happening at a school, such as a field trip, special event, etc.
Wednesday	#WayBackWednesday—historical photos and facts
	#WednesdayWisdom—famous quote to inspire or maybe one from a student
Thursday	#ThrowBackThursday—historical photos and facts
	#ThankfulThursday—gratitude for staff, families, community
Friday	#FridayNightFootball—ask them to post highlights and photos from the game
	#FridayFunday—similar to #MondayFunday, show pics of your staff having fun, or it can be more open to sharing anything fun
	#FollowFriday—tag and highlight other organizations worth following
	#FlashBackFriday—similar to #ThrowbackThursday, follows the same theme of sharing old pics

Potential Contests

Contests are a proven method of increasing engagement on social media platforms and building followers. Below are several examples of contests that could be implemented at the school or district level. Prizes could include district or school gear or even donations from area businesses that could be tagged as sponsors, increasing reach for both the district and the local business.

Photo Asks—Consider asking your online community to send in photos regarding a specific theme. Consider having a "photo ask" campaign each month. For example, in July and August, try a summer holidays album where the community is able to send in photos and stories of what they are doing for summer travel and activities. These campaigns can lead to a major increase in engagement because entire families can be tagged and the post reaches all of their friends as well.

Voting Add-Ons—You can ask your followers to vote on their favorite submissions by "liking" them and award the poster who has the most likes at the conclusion of the contest.

Write a Caption—They submit and vote on captions (titles) for photos that you post. These contests are a great contest idea to engage fans. They often stimulate competition when entrants get passionate.

Biggest Fans—Challenge your followers to submit a photo that shows just how much they love a teacher or your school or district. This is also a great way to collect some great photos and stories to reuse individually at some time in the future.

Check-Ins—Ask your families to check in on Facebook for a particular event, such as an open house, then award a prize based on a drawing at the end of a specific time period.

Trivia—Ask a trivia question about your school or district or an interest area that appeals to your followers. Then offer a small prize to whoever correctly answers the question first.

Guessing Games—Set up a guessing game and award a prize to the person who answers correctly or gets the closest. Similar to "How many jellybeans are in this jar?" but make it more relevant to education like the number of Chromebooks or smartboards in the district.

There are also some regular events and content areas that schools are leading discussions about each year. Take those discussions online, for example:

- Favorite or outstanding teacher/nurse/counselor/custodian/bus driver/vice-principal/principal/coach
- Grandparent Day photo and essay

- Arts video or photo of experience or piece
- Math/STEM experience with photo or video
- Good study habits or test-taking tips
- Good news at your school/school spirit/character education
- Disability awareness
- June summer-learning experience
- Fourth of July celebration, democracy, and education
- Favorite books of the summer; lists for grade levels or classes
- August—"What excites you about returning to school?"
- A welcoming moment at your school
- Internet safety/training

Reinforce Tone

It is important to develop a real "voice" that is consistent across platforms, tools, and materials. In essence, your stakeholder groups should be able to recognize your school or district tone the way they could identify the tone of a person they know.

In conjunction with staying true to tone, be a good social media citizen. Engage with other organizations, school districts, people, and businesses. Engage and expand with their posts and link to other organization's blogs, videos, and news articles. Retweet what others have to say as a way of reinforcing common messages and demonstrating good online behavior for families.

Practical Management Issues

The less exciting side of social media is thinking through the administrative tasks that will keep it successful. It doesn't have to be a lot of ongoing work. Deciding and implementing a few things annually can save a lot of time during the rest of the year.

Best posting times—Looking at the engagement data trends is the best way to determine the best times to post. If your posts on a certain day and time are getting more attention, that's the time to post!

Repost, reuse, recycle—Keep track of your content for the year and hold onto it for the coming years. While you'll want to switch out the photos or videos, you can post something fairly similar at the same time next year without anyone really noticing.

Develop guidelines—Make sure staff knows what the boundaries are for participating in the official social media accounts. They will evolve as new social networking tools emerge.

Content calendar—Make social media easier to manage by building an annual social media calendar that shares content from your other sources (website, newspaper, etc.), communicates about important events and deadlines (graduations, SATs, financial aid, etc.), and allows for some spontaneity. See Table 12.1 earlier in the chapter for a brief example.

Audience analysis—Understand what your target audience is talking about and connect to them on those issues rather than only posting what is in your school or district interest.

Interns—If there are high schoolers in the school or district that can be trusted, recruit them to help take on the social media content and add a student voice. Interview students who are interested, establish solid rules, and provide account access on a device owned and located at the school or district.

Civility policy—Make sure that you've created and listed a civility policy. Visit the social media profile of a district you admire and you'll likely find one there. The policy will point to expectations and consequences when online behavior of followers doesn't live up to the policy. It's important to be direct but not too negative.

Know your why—Understand why you are adopting a new social media platform. Table 12.3 outlines key questions to ask when considering adding a new tool.

Assigning access—Make sure it is a general school profile that can be passed on to the next administrator rather than a specific person so that the school or district always has a way to access the account.

Images and video—When you post a photo or video connected to the topic, audience engagement is much higher. They don't have to be polished; in fact, there is a lot of charm to something created by a student or teacher that isn't quite perfect. Just make sure that the photos you take or receive from third parties do not show students that have opted out of school or district photos and promotion.

Links—These can be tricky if they are not from trusted sources. Ensure that the site you are sending people to meets school or district content standards. If it's a good landing spot for families, test links to make sure they are working and then delete the link text after you see the thumbnail appear.

Spelling and grammar—Most platforms have built-in spell checking; however, if you have a question about your content, write it out in Word or Google Docs to ensure it is without errors. The public is not very forgiving of educational agency spelling and grammatical errors. When possible, have someone else review your post to check for tone and accuracy.

Table 12.3.

General	• What will the new platform add to your communication and engagement efforts? • Will it replace an existing platform, or is it a completely new addition? • Are there any district or state policies or regulations associated with the functionality of this platform? • What are the potential risks associated with the use of this platform, and how are you mitigating these risks?
Content Providers	• How many staff will have access to the platform as content providers? • How many staff will be expected to post content on this platform? • What is the learning curve for this platform? • Will there be a review of posts by an administrator?
Audience	• How many employees, families, or students currently use this platform? • How many employees, families, or students would potentially use this platform? • How do you know this?
Platform Content	• How often will you be posting using this platform? • What kind of content will be posted on this platform?
Training	• How many users would need to be trained on the new platform? • Is there training available?
Access	• Will the platform log-in be set up so that district level and other administrators can get into the platform? • Will the platform belong to the department or campus and be passed to the next leadership team?

IN SUMMARY

The chapters in this book are an effort to show the value of data as well as to provide simple and easy ideas for a data-driven approach to school communication. Research, measuring, and evaluation are not only for researchers; it is also for anyone with limited time and resources who wants to maximize their efforts. It doesn't have to take a lot of extra funding, but it does take some curiosity, creativity, and an open mind.

It would be a mistake to think that this book is an argument that data can solve all issues. While there are a number of highly valuable things that data can do for a school or district leader, there are very important things that data can't do. Data can't calm an upset parent, and it can't build better relationships. Data can't increase trust with stakeholders, and it can't keep you personally healthy and balanced.

When used effectively, data *can* help you understand the why behind communication and focus on impact so you have more time for those things that need your personal attention.

KEY IDEAS IN THIS CHAPTER

- There are many systemic ways to ensure that communication is a part of everyone's job.
- Social media is an important tool to help connect with families, and there are simple ways to reduce the amount of content schools have to produce to keep up.
- Data can't solve all problems, but it can free up time to apply personal talents to other challenges.

CASE STUDY 12.1—SOCIAL MEDIA AND E-NEWSLETTERS ARE A TEAM EFFORT

Escalon Unified, a rural six-school district in California, isn't large enough to fund a full-time communication director. Superintendent Ron Costa hasn't let that fact stop them from reaching out to families in every way possible.

Through an annual communication preference survey, stakeholders told the district that one the main areas that could be improved was the use of Facebook and the addition of a monthly digital newsletter. There was just one problem: no one at the district office felt confident enough to get them started.

They used a communication consultant to create the district Facebook page and to create the e-newsletter template. Costa met with his principals and created a monthly schedule for Facebook posts and e-newsletters, asking each school to submit one post a month and two articles a year.

Their Facebook page has shared photos, videos, and stories from classrooms around the district and boasts a healthy following of more than six hundred as of the writing of this book. Their e-newsletter is also going strong, providing additional Facebook post teaser articles that lead people back to the full e-newsletter.

In the follow-up survey, stakeholders commented on the new outreach tools and awareness in all categories went up. An unintended benefit is the delight it is bringing to staff. Each month, a certified and classified staff member is honored, and a story is posted in both the e-newsletter and on Facebook.

The community response to the posts has been overwhelmingly positive, bringing current parents, staff, and alumni together in celebration of the "spotlight" employees.

Appendix A

Communications Plan Example

Problem/Challenge/Opportunity:
(Keep it at a high level, one or two sentences)
[ABC Unified School District has created a new STEM program that will help keep advanced math and science students in our district]

Situation Analysis:
(What do we know based on the research? Don't forget to include what you know about audience information preferences)
- [Example - According to internal tracking of trends the past five years, our enrollment is declining at an alarming rate]
- [Example – According to our last communication survey, most of our families have access to the internet and prefer to be contacted by email]

Goals:
(Broad goals for overall plan – audience specific objectives come later)
[Promote awareness of new STEM program and increase enrollment at XYZ High School]

Audience 1 _____ *(Repeat for each audience)*
[Example – Middle school families, local real estate agents, PTA leaders, all families, elementary teachers, board members]

Messages:
- [Example -Our new STEM program will prepare students for college and career paths]
- [Example – Our STEM program is open to all ABC Unified students & students in neighboring districts]
- [Example – Our STEM program will feature new hands-on labs and one-to-one technology access]

Objective Target: _____ *(repeat for each objective)*
(Increase/Decrease/Establish Baseline/Execute/Implement + Awareness/Knowledge/Attendance/Responses/Event + by % or # on or before Date)
[Example – Increase awareness of the STEM program by 30% based on post campaign survey on or before May 2017]
[Example – Implement new board policy to allow neighboring students to attend STEM program on or before January 2017]
[Example – Establish baseline awareness of STEM program on or before December 2016]

Objective Actual: _____ *(repeat for each objective after tactics are completed and results are in)*

[Example – Increased awareness of the STEM program by 30% based on post campaign survey in April 2017]

Tactics/Tools	Responsible	Budget	Deadline	Output
[Example – Create and Send enewsletter on STEM program to elementary families	Trinette	$30	Nov 2016	# sent, opens, clicks

Objective Target: _____ (repeat for each objective)
(Increase/Decrease/Establish Baseline/Execute/Implement + Awareness/Knowledge/Attendance/Responses/Event + by % or # on or before Date)
[Example – Increase awareness of the STEM program by 30% based on post campaign survey on or before May 2017]
[Example – Implement new board policy to allow neighboring students to attend STEM program on or before January 2017]
[Example – Establish baseline awareness of STEM program on or before December 2016]

Objective Actual: _____ [repeat for each objective after tactics are completed and results are in]
[Example – Increased awareness of the STEM program by 30% based on post campaign survey in April 2017]

Tactics/Tools	Responsible	Budget	Deadline	Output
[Example – Create and Send enewsletter on STEM program to elementary families	Trinette	$30	Nov 2016	# sent, opens, clicks

Audience 2 _____ *(Repeat for each audience)*
[Example – Middle school families, local real estate agents, PTA leaders, all families, elementary teachers, board members]

Messages:
- [Example –Our new STEM program will prepare students for college and career paths]
- [Example – Our STEM program is open to all ABC Unified students & students in neighboring districts]
- [Example – Our STEM program will feature new hands-on labs and one-to-one technology access]

Objective Target: _____ (repeat for each objective)
(Increase/Decrease/Establish Baseline/Execute/Implement + Awareness/Knowledge/Attendance/Responses/Event + by % or # on or before Date)
[Example – Increase awareness of the STEM program by 30% based on campaign survey on or before May 2017]
[Example – Implement new board policy to allow neighboring students to attend STEM program on or before January 2017]
[Example – Establish baseline awareness of STEM program on or before December 2016]

Objective Actual: _____ (repeat for each objective after tactics are completed and results are in)
[Example – Increased awareness of the STEM program by 30% based on post campaign survey in April 2017]

Tactics/Tools	Responsible	Budget	Deadline	Output
[Example – Create and Send enewsletter on STEM program to elementary families	Trinette	$30	Nov 2016	# sent, opens, clicks

Objective Target: _____ (repeat for each objective)
(Increase/Decrease/Establish Baseline/Execute/Implement + Awareness/Knowledge/Attendance/Responses/Event + by % or # on or before Date)
[Example – Increase awareness of the STEM program by 30% based on campaign survey on or before May 2017]
[Example – Implement new board policy to allow neighboring students to attend STEM program on or before January 2017]
[Example – Establish baseline awareness of STEM program on or before December 2016]

Objective Actual: _____ (repeat for each objective after tactics are completed and results are in)
[Example – Increased awareness of the STEM program by 30% based on post campaign survey in April 2017]

Tactics/Tools	Responsible	Budget	Deadline	Output
[Example – Create and Send enewsletter on STEM program to elementary families	Trinette	$30	Nov 2016	# sent, opens, clicks

Audience 3 _____ *(Repeat for each audience)*
[Example – Middle school families, local real estate agents, PTA leaders, all families, elementary teachers, board members]

Messages:
- [Example -Our new STEM program will prepare students for college and career paths]
- [Example – Our STEM program is open to all ABC Unified students & students in neighboring districts]
- [Example – Our STEM program will feature new hands-on labs and one-to-one technology access]

Objective Target: _____ *(repeat for each objective)*
(Increase/Decrease/Establish Baseline/Execute/Implement + Awareness/Knowledge/Attendance/Responses/Event + by % or # on or before Date)
[Example – Increase awareness of the STEM program by 30% based on post campaign survey on or before May 2017]
[Example – Implement new board policy to allow neighboring students to attend STEM program on or before January 2017]
[Example – Establish baseline awareness of STEM program on or before December 2016]

Objective Actual: _____ *(repeat for each objective after tactics are completed and results are in)*
[Example – Increased awareness of the STEM program by 30% based on post campaign survey in April 2017]

Tactics/Tools	Responsible	Budget	Deadline	Output
[Example – Create and Send enewsletter on STEM program to elementary families	Trinette	$30	Nov 2016	# sent, opens, clicks

Objective Target: _____ *(repeat for each objective)*
(Increase/Decrease/Establish Baseline/Execute/Implement + Awareness/Knowledge/Attendance/Responses/Event + by % or # on or before Date)
[Example – Increase awareness of the STEM program by 30% based on post campaign survey on or before May 2017]
[Example – Implement new board policy to allow neighboring students to attend STEM program on or before January 2017]
[Example – Establish baseline awareness of STEM program on or before December 2016]

Objective Actual: _____ *(repeat for each objective after tactics are completed and results are in)*
[Example – Increased awareness of the STEM program by 30% based on post campaign survey in April 2017]

Tactics/Tools	Responsible	Budget	Deadline	Output
[Example – Create and Send enewsletter on STEM program to elementary families	Trinette	$30	Nov 2016	# sent, opens, clicks

Appendix B

Sample Communication Survey Questions

QUANTITATIVE QUESTIONS

1. How would you rate your knowledge of the following aspects of the ABC Public Schools? (1=Not very knowledgeable, 5=Very knowledgeable)

   - Mission
   - Plans
   - Policies
   - Events
   - Accomplishments
   - Day-to-day operations
   - Challenges

2. Please select each of the ways you have received information about ABC Public Schools:

   - District website
   - School website
   - Automated calls
   - School emails
   - District emails
   - Local media
   - School Facebook page
   - District Facebook page
   - School Twitter account
   - District Twitter account

3. Please rate the effectiveness of the communication tools in ABC USD. Please skip the methods you haven't used. (1=Not very effective, 5=Very effective)

   - District website
   - School website
   - Automated calls
   - School emails
   - District emails
   - Local media
   - School Facebook page
   - District Facebook page
   - School Twitter account
   - District Twitter account

4. Which best describes your impression of communications within the ABC Public Schools?

   - Doesn't tell us much about what's going on.
   - Gives us a limited amount of information.
   - Keeps us adequately informed.
   - Keeps us fairly well-informed.
   - Keeps us fully informed.

5. Please rate the level of trust you have in ABC Public Schools to do the following (1=Very low level of trust, 5=Very high level of trust):

   - Create a safe, welcoming, and nurturing learning environment
   - Conduct business with transparency and open communication
   - Develop a collaborative and respectful working environments
   - Inspire each student to achieve career and college success

6. How does your level of trust in ABC Public Schools this year compare with your level of trust last year?

   - My level of trust is about the same as last year.
   - My level of trust has improved since last year.
   - My level of trust has decreased since last year.

QUALITATIVE QUESTIONS

Three open-ended questions to solicit ideas from respondents on the best communication practices, how to improve communication, and specific tools they believe the district should be using more often. The analysis involves reading all of the responses, categorizing them, and identifying top themes.

- What is the best thing about communication in ABC Public Schools?
- How would you improve communication in ABC Public Schools?
- Are there any specific communication tools you think we should be using or using more often?

Appendix C

Training Ideas to Expand Communications Function

Even if your district has a large PR department, it's a good idea to provide a variety of training to ensure that everyone sees good communication as part of their job each day.

Customer Service—Marketing efforts fall flat if the student, family, or staff experience isn't a good one. Customer service is a skill that needs to be refreshed from time to time.

Creating a Welcoming Place for English-Language Learner Families—When your district demographics are changing and your staff doesn't look like the students you serve, a specialized customer service course highlighting cultural issues can bring people together.

Branding—Review your school or district strengths and communication practices that build support for your school.

Media Training—Best practices and tips for receiving more positive attention with less effort.

Public Speaking—Key training for administrators who don't yet feel confident leading a large public meeting.

Crisis Communication—Build key relationships and establish roles before a crisis hits so everyone is prepared.

Family and Community Engagement—How to engage parents with your school or district in a meaningful way.

Smartphone Video Production—Make exciting and inspiring videos of classroom learning using a simple smartphone and a few gadgets and apps.

Social Media—Set the expectations for tone and participation and provide creative content tips.

School and Teacher Website Expectations—Best practices to ensure quality websites at all levels.

Appendix D

Four-Step Process Campaign Example—Increasing Free and Reduced Meal Applications

Located just east of Sacramento, San Juan Unified School District serves a very diverse population—many walks of life are represented, from recent immigrants from the Middle East to sons and daughters of prominent politicians and everything in between.

In 2017, leaders in the district began to suspect that schools and families were not receiving all of the resources they should due to the lack of demonstrated need to the state. Under current law, the needs must be demonstrated through free and reduced meal application approval. Even if a student does not plan to eat meals through the program, demonstrating the need for additional resources helps the family and the school in many other ways.

Also, with fewer resources available, San Juan was forced to take funds from other sources to meet critical needs. This meant less money available for programs, teachers, staff, and students throughout the district.

RESEARCH

The community relations, nutrition services, and curriculum and instruction departments teamed up to find out more about the issue. They started with the California Longitudinal Pupil Achievement Data System (CALPADS), a system used to maintain individual-level data, including student demographics, course data, discipline, assessments, staff assignments, and other data for state and federal reporting.

The most relevant information from CALPADS for a potential campaign included the total number of students, how many qualified for free or reduced lunch, and how many were English-language learners (ELLs)—all key indicators for state funding.

They also reviewed the research and results from a neighboring district that had conducted a similar campaign. One lesson learned from that campaign was to broaden the messaging and make it about more than lunches. Another was to make sure the campaign used multiple methods for reaching families.

PLANNING/ANALYSIS

As a result of the research, they set an objective to raise the students qualifying for free and reduced meals by at least 4.8 percent to help San Juan meet the California Local Control Accountability Formula minimum.

When 55 percent of a district's population is certified as eligible to receive free and reduced meals, districts receive additional flexibility in the use of funds. If they maintain a 55 percent demonstrated need for three years, districts receive additional funding from the state to address student needs.

It was an especially lofty objective given the political climate. With a new federal administration that had a completely different perspective and rhetoric on immigration, districts throughout California were hearing talk about families being afraid to participate in a USDA program. They were afraid that putting their information on a federal form and accepting benefits would affect their status in the country.

Many districts were concerned that these fears would keep families from participating in the program—which would mean many kids would go hungry and schools would lose out on funding for the needs that were in the classroom.

San Juan's plan involved a lot more than traditional communication channels. They reviewed the entire free and reduced meal process, inviting representatives from each of the district departments that had any involvement in the application. In their bi-weekly meetings, they broke down each step in the process and identified any barriers to submitting an application along the way.

The key audiences included families but also site administration and staff. The planning group understood that if site and department staff didn't understand the bigger picture and the reason for the push, they would be less likely to give the campaign the attention it needed to succeed.

As for messaging, the feeling was that the entire free and reduced meal application concept needed to be refreshed. The process documents district-wide need and affects resources in many areas, and the messaging needed to reflect that.

As a result, the key messages included:

- The applications have a positive financial impact for schools.
- There are non-meal benefits to families.
- It is easy and secure to apply.

More specifically, the tagline for the campaign became "more than a meal" and explained the various benefits to schools and individuals, such as reduced prices on the internet, bus passes, and college applications.

COMMUNICATION/IMPLEMENTATION

The campaign strategies included reworking the application process to make it flow better and using a variety of tactics, including standard mailing and forms, to ensure the word got out. The process became integrated with online school registration, which made it easy to fill out and hard to ignore since families had to "opt out" of filling out the application.

A new webpage was created to explain the importance of the application with links to the online application, school resource impact examples, and non-meal benefits for families. A new graphic was also created to communicate all the benefits in a way that was easily understood.

San Juan also took advantage of existing communication opportunities to get the word out. Principals and staff were briefed at regional meetings and received discussion points about the campaign. They were encouraged to discuss the campaign at student and family meetings and orientations.

Families received a series of automated calls and texts; information was listed on digital school signs and in district internal and external publications. The annual nutrition services mailing included the new benefit graphic and additional information about why returning the application was important even if they didn't think their family would qualify.

EVALUATION

San Juan had set an objective to raise the students qualifying for free and reduced meals by at least 4.8 percent to help San Juan meet the California Local Control Accountability Formula minimum of 55 percent. At the end of the five-month campaign, the results were impressive and were more importantly good for students and families.

As of the CALPADs census date, 21,522 students qualified for free or reduced lunch, up 5.2 percent (1,552 students) to 55.4 percent.

What is behind the numbers is even more powerful—as a result of the collaborative effort involving nearly every department, San Juan has more information about the real needs of their students. They'll be feeding more kids, getting families access to more services, and because they surpassed the 55 percent threshold, they'll have more flexibility in how to do it. Also, if they are able to document the same levels of need for an additional two years, they'll receive more funding overall.

Appendix E

Communication Options Worksheet

Communication Options Worksheet – Proactively communicate your campus changes, events, information

Issue _____

Messaging _____

Type	Audience	Responsible	Deadline	Completed
Automated Phone Call/text	Families, staff			
Web Site –News/Calendar	General public			
Campus Sign	Families, community			
Letter or Flyer Sent home/mailed	Staff and families			
Discussion at Advisory Meeting	Families			
Staff Email	Staff (don't forget classified!)			
Discussion at Staff Meeting	Staff			
Posters around Campus	Families, students, staff			
Discussion Points Drafted for meetings/trainings	Staff, families			
Press Release or Advisory Sent to local media	Media and general public			
Social Media Facebook, Twitter, YouTube				
Rep to District Advisory Group	District staff			
District Communication Tools	Varies			

Communication Options Worksheet – Proactively communicate your campus changes, events, information

Issue _____

Messaging _____
_____

Type	Audience	Responsible	Deadline	Completed

Glossary

List of related communication terms with a definition of how they are being used in this book.

Anecdotal—a specific incidence that may or may not be representative of a larger group
Audiences—the key people that need to receive the message to make the campaign successful
Campaign—collection of activities based on research and planning that are designed to create change
Channel—specific way of communicating something, usually related to a communication tool
Collateral—materials that are created to support a campaign
Content provider—anyone that is contributing a video, photo or text in the messaging of a campaign
Convenience—in research sampling, it is when you ask whoever is easiest to ask
Engagement—two-way communication, interaction with the message or sender
Evaluative—research that helps evaluate how successful a campaign is
Formal—research that can be replicated with similar results
Formative—research that helps in deciding what to do in a campaign or tests messages before they are sent
Impressions—times that a message is viewed
Informal—research that is difficult to replicate, not random
Measurable objective—set goal for the change you want to see in a PR campaign
Message—words or images communicated out as part of the campaign

Primary—when you or your organization do the research
Respondent—someone who replies to a survey
Secondary—when someone else did the research
Protocol—list of agreed-upon guidelines for a process
Qualitative—information that helps with understanding the nature of something
Quantitative—information that can be added and helps with understanding the scope of something
Reach—how many people have been exposed to the message
Representative—when something applies to the experience or perception of a larger group
Stakeholders—all the people and groups that interact with the school community in some way
Strategy—type of activity that is part of a communications campaign
Tactic—specific activity that is part of a communications campaign
Tool—computer program, app, or voice messaging system that assists with disseminating content
Tracking—collecting data about communication activities

Resources

Looking for additional information on one of the topics covered in this book? Here are a few organizations, books, and websites that may help.

PUBLIC RELATIONS AND COMMUNICATION RESOURCES

National School Public Relations Association (www.nspra.org): School communication training and services through an annual seminar, monthly webinars, and e-newsletters

NSPRA Books and Resources (www.nspra.org/products): Online store of books and other materials supporting school communication

State-Based School Public Relations Associations (nspra.org/nspra-chapters): There are thirty-three state-sponsored chapters of NSPRA that offer local school communication training and support.

Public Relations Society of America (www.prsa.org): Offers general public relations professional development and support.

Accreditation in Public Relations (prsa.org/learning/accreditation): Accreditation in Public Relations is a voluntary certification program for public relations professionals.

SOCIAL MEDIA RESOURCES

Embracing Social Media: A Practical Guide to Manage Risk and Leverage Opportunity, by Kristin Magette: Book focused on school social media practices and tips

https://www.socialmediaexaminer.com/: Website with general social media advice and training

https://sproutsocial.com/: Website with general social media advice and training

https://hootsuite.com/: Website with general social media advice and training

CONNECTING

I love sharing knowledge and connecting with others working to improve school communication; feel free to reach out or take advantage of the stuff on my website.

http://www.schoolprpro.com: Additional electronic versions of templates, online trainings, recordings, and monthly podcasts

Email: Trinette@schoolprpro.com
Twitter: @trinettemarquis
LinkedIn: linkedin.com/in/trinettemarquis

About the Author

With more than twenty years of experience in communications, marketing, and public relations, **Trinette Marquis** is passionate about working with public schools and improving school community relationships. Early in her career, she cut her teeth with Fortune 500 companies, statewide nonprofits, and internet start-ups, but she came to the realization that something was missing. Inspired by her father's positive experience as a custodian, Trinette brought her business talents to the schools where she grew up and eventually started her own consulting firm to help districts throughout the country.

Her work has been recognized by the National School Public Relations Association, Medical Marketing Association, and the International Association of Business Communicators. In 2010, she was awarded the National Leadership through Communication Award by the American Association of School Administrators. She is a past president of the California School Public Relations Association and presents regularly to national audiences. She also enjoys teaching locally as a part-time professor of communications at California State University, Sacramento. She holds a master's degree in organizational communication and is accredited in public relations. When she's not teaching or consulting, you can find Trinette hiking around northern California with her family.

www.ingramcontent.com/pod-product-compliance
Lightning Source LLC
Chambersburg PA
CBHW030142240426
43672CB00005B/239